Instant Omni Plus Air Fryer Toast Oven Cookbook 2020-2021

Enjoy Easy Tasty Recipes on A Budget for Anybody Who Want to Improve Living

By Dane Larsen

Table of contents

Introduction

The latest and possibly most awesome appliance of the Instant Family is out in the market. It has already started to take the whole world by storm!

While most other Toaster Oven's boast their compact size, in reality, they are very small for large families, despite packing a lot of features.

The Instant Omni Plus Air Fryer Toaster Oven is the solution to all of these problems! Not only does this appliance pack a wide variety of different smart programs for you choose from, but it also boasts a whopping 26L internal capacity, which makes this the perfect appliance for large families alike.

The versatility of this appliance will allow you to Roast, Air Fry, Bake, Toast, Slow Cook, and a lot more!

This particular book has been designed to act as an entry point into the world of Omni Plus, and as such, the first chapter of the book tries to cover some of the most fundamental concepts of the Omni appliance that you should know about

And once you are done with the basics, you will find a plethora of 100+ stunning recipes for you to enjoy! Recipes are categorized based on ingredient type as well as special functions, so you will easily be able to find what you are looking for.

So, don't waste any more time and jump right in!

Bon Appetit!

Chapter 1: The Fundamentals Of Omni Plus Air Fryer Toaster Oven

What is Instant Omni Plus Air Fryer Toaster Oven

The Instant Omni Plus Toaster Oven Air Fryer is possibly one of the most innovative and versatile cooking appliances to date that offers a wide variety of cooking options to choose from, alongside having a large capacity, which is a combination that most previous toaster ovens have failed to do.

The size alone is one of the key selling factors of this amazing appliance, which is a whopping 26L!

But apart from the capacity, the Omni Plus Toaster Oven can Bake, Roast, Dehydrate, Toast, and even Air Fry under the same hood! And that's not even all. There are more than 8 different smart cooking options for you to choose from.

Functions of the Omni Plus Toaster Oven

While using the Omni Toaster Oven is extremely easy to use, having a good understanding of the different buttons and functions of the appliance will help you better understand how the appliance works.

The core functions are as listed below:

Air Fry: This function is used to Air Fryer meals. You can use to prepare oil-free crispy meals with ease alongside being able to bring a nice caramelized finish to your cooked dishes.

Toast: This will allow you to your Omni to Toast bread alongside various other meals.

Bake: The bake mode is used to particularly prepare cake, cookies, brownies, muffins pizza, etc. alongside other various meals.

Broil: If you are looking to simply brown the top of your dessert or casserole, the Broil function is what you need.

Roast: This function is used to roast vegetables,s meat, and even whole chicken.

Slow Cook: This function will allow you to cook meals at a very low temperature and for a prolonged period. It keeps the food warm and preserves all the nutritional values of the meal.

Reheat: This function is best when you want to simply re-heat your leftover.

Proof: In this mode, the appliance uses the halogen lighting to keep the inside of your oven warm. This allows yeas to rise during the proofing process.

Dehydrate: This function is used to dehydrate fruits/veggie meat slices for preservation.

Convect And Rotate: These two are cooking methods that are used for cooking whole chicken type meals with the help of the rotisserie spit and forks.

Advantages of the Omni Toaster Oven

There some absolutely amazing advantages to the Omni Toaster Oven that you should know about!

- The carefully designed enclosure of the appliance is one the safest cooking appliance out there, it completely eliminates the risk of oil spitting out and falling in your skin.
- Since you will not be using that much oil, there will be very little grease build-up, which in turn will make the appliance very easy to clean
- The Omni Plus Air Fryer Toaster Oven is an amazing and versatile appliance that has 10+ cooking features under its hood. With just a single appliance, you can dehydrate, proof, reheat, slow cooker, roast, Air Fry, and a lot more!
- Since this appliance utilizes air when it comes to Air Frying, you will be saving a lot of time in the kitchen
- The Omni Toaster Oven really makes meals healthier as it cuts down almost 80-85% of the oil required to make dishes. In the long run, this will greatly improve your health

And those were just the most crucial ones, there are lots more!

Accessories and construction of the appliance

All the smart programs of Instant Omni are customizable. Even when the cooking program is running, the settings can be changed using the temperature and time knobs. The adjustable programs allow the users to switch from one cooking settings to another with its super flexible heating system.

Even-Heat: Toasts Both Sides Due to its convection heating mechanism, the Instant Omni toaster oven is capable of heating the food from all sides. This feature ensures even heating. When bread slices or bagels are toasted inside this toaster oven, they are cooked both from the top and the bottom. Without flipping a single slice, a user can get evenly cooked and crispy toasts.

When it comes to electric appliances, it is important to inspect all the parts of the appliance before giving it a test run. The Instant Omni toaster oven comes with the following basic elements and the accessories.

- The Oven Base unit
- Rack tray
- Crumb Tray
- Oven Door
- Rotisserie Catch

- Rotisserie Spit & Forks Rotisserie Lift
- Air Fry Basket
- Baking pan
- Baking trays
- Power plug

Inside the Instant Omni plus oven, there are three grooves on both sides. These grooves are used to insert three rack trays in the oven. The uppermost grooves can be used to insert the trays when the food needs to be broiled. The center grooves are for Air frying and Roasting purposes. The lowermost level is used to place the food which needs to be baked, reheated, or dehydrated. Crumb tray is inserted at the bottom to protect the bottom of the oven from the food particle during cooking.

The rotisserie stick can be inserted and used to fix the meat of chicken. This stick can be fixed on the inner side of the center portion of the oven into the rotisserie catch. Air fryer basket can be placed on the lower rack when required.

Cleaning And Maintenance Instructions

It is highly recommended that you try to properly clean up your Omni Plus Toaster Oven after every use to keep it free from germs and other harmful dirt and debris. It might often happen that after you are done cooking, some dirt and debris might stay stuck into the Omni Toaster Oven wall. The simple and easy steps below will help you deal with these issues and keep your appliance in tip-top shape.

- Before starting your cleaning process, make sure to unplug the Omni Plus from the socket, open the bay door and let it cool until it reaches room temperature
- Remove all the accessories from inside like drip pan, steel rack, air fryer basket, rotisserie, etc.
- Keep in mind that all the accessories used by the Toaster Oven are completely dishwasher safe, you can easily wash them by putting them into your dishwasher and drying them out completely
- Once you are done with that, clean the oven from the inside by using a clean and damp cloth. Carefully clean all the inner walls using a cloth
- Once you are done with the inner body, clean the exterior by using a damp cloth
- Clean both the display and the touch buttons with a soft cloth
- Assemble the removable parts like the steel rack, dripping pan and other accessories back into the original position
- Check the cable for any damage, clean it wit ha dry cloth

And just like, Your Omni is now ready for next use!

Hearty Tips for the appliance

Below are some hearty tips that will help you along the way:

- If you simply press the temperature knob for about 3 seconds, the temperature scale will shift from Celsius to Fahrenheit. If you hold it again, it will go back to Fahrenheit
- If you hold the time knob for 3 seconds, it will tur on the oven light
- If you want to cancel the default settings of the modes, simply hold the cancel button for 3 seconds
- If you want to deactivate the beeping sound, hold the temperature and time knob at the same time. You will see a message "SOFF" displayed, this means that the sound is off. If you repeat it again and hold both buttons for 3 seconds, the sound will come back.
- Always try to clean your Omni Toaster Oven after every use
- If you want the best air circulation, lower your baking tray to the middle position
- Make sure unplug your appliance when you are not using it anymore
- Make sure to never put anything on top of the appliance while using it, as it would affect the temperature gauge

Awesome Meal Prep Ideas

Below are some of the most simple meal prep ideas that you can seamlessly combine with your very own Omni Plus so that you can prepare your meals ahead of time.

Keep your prepared smoothies frozen in muffin tins: Plopping out some different ingredients early in the morning might be a chore for some people. A simple solution to that is to go ahead and freeze up your blended smoothies in muffin tins. This will not only save up time but will also give you a good dose of satisfaction as you wake up in the morning and toss a few "smoothie cups" into the blender for a simple yet healthy breakfast.

Roast vegetables that require the same time in one batch: When you are preparing large batches of vegetables for roasting, it is smart to go ahead and create batches of vegetables depending on how long they take to roast. For example, you can create a batch of rapid cooking vegetables such as mushrooms, asparagus, or cherry tomatoes and a batch of slow roasting veggies such as potatoes, cauliflowers, and carrots to minimize time loss and maximize output.

Make a plan ahead of time: If you have this book on your hand, then you are surely an extremely busy man/woman and are looking for a way to incorporate a healthy lifestyle into your hectic routine, right? Well, the first step to that is to prepare a well-organized Meal Plan. The primary purpose of the Meal Plan will be to provide you an approximate outline of the meals that you are going to prepare for the coming week. This will help you to do your shopping early and prepare them accordingly. During the early days, I would recommend that you keep 2 days a week for prepping and the remaining days of eating.

Keep a good supply of mason jars: Mason jars are terrific, not only for storing memories! But also for storing healthy salads! Assuming that you are a good buff, it might be a good idea to prepare your salads ahead of time and store them in mason jars. Make sure to keep the salad dressing at the bottom of the jar to ensure that nothing greens don't get soggy!

Three-way seasoning in one pan: If you want to stick to lean meats such as chicken, then an excellent way to season multiple batches and prepare them beforehand is to keep them in the same container while separating them using aluminum foil. Using these will allow you to season three or more (depending on how many dividers you are using) types of chicken seasoning to be done using the same pan!

Chapter 2: Breakfast

Morning Quinoa Bread

Bread made of Quinoa? Who would've thought that anything like that was even possible right? But here it is! A healthy treat right in your hand.

Prep time and cooking time: 40 minutes | Serves: 4

Ingredients To Use:

- 1 and 3/4 cups uncooked quinoa, soaked and overnight, rinsed
- 1/4 cup sesame seeds
- 1/2 teaspoon baking soda
- 1/4 teaspoon salt
- 1/4 cup olive oil
- 1/2 cup of sparkling water
- 1 tablespoon fresh lemon juice

Step-by-Step Directions to cook it:

1. Preheat your Omni Toaster Oven to 300 degrees F in Air Fry mode
2. Line loaf pan with parchment paper
3. Take a food processor and add all ingredients, pulse well
4. Transfer into the pan and transfer pan to cooking basket
5. Cook for 30-40 minutes until a toothpick comes clean
6. Remove pan from Fryer and keep in the cooling rack, let it cool
7. Serve and enjoy!

Nutritional value per serving:

Calories: 140 kcal, Protein: 14g, Fat: 7g, Carbs: 16g

Baked Okra And Tomato Delight

Nothing can beat the freshness of a mix of tomato and Okra together in a platter. This is a great way to start your day!
Prep time and cooking time: 90 minutes | Serves: 4

Ingredients To Use:

- 1/2 cup lime beans, frozen
- 4 tomatoes, chopped
- 8 ounces okra, fresh and washed, stemmed, sliced into 1/2 inch thick slices
- 1 onion, sliced into rings
- 1/2 sweet pepper, seeded and sliced thin
- Pinch of crushed red pepper
- Salt to taste

Step-by-Step Directions to cook it:

1. Preheat your Omni Toaster Oven to 350 degrees F in Bake Mode
2. Cook Lime beans in water accordingly and drain them, take a 2-quarter casserole tin
3. Add all listed Ingredients the dish and cover with foil, bake for 45 minutes
4. Uncover the dish, stir well and bake for 35 minutes more
5. Give it a final stir, serve and enjoy!

Nutritional value per serving:

Calories: 55 kcal, Protein: 3g, Fat: 0g, Carbs: 12g

Zucchini Zoodles And Avocado Sauce

Looking for noodles but want to stay on the healthy side? Try out the zoodles with tasty avocado sauce, you are gonna love it!
Prep time and cooking time: 30 minutes | Serves: 4

Ingredients To Use:

- 3 medium zucchini
- 1 and 1/2 cup cherry tomatoes
- 1 avocado
- 2 green onions, sliced
- 1 garlic clove
- 3 tablespoons olive oil
- Juice of 1 key lemon
- 1 tablespoon spring water
- Salt and cayenne to taste

Step-by-Step Directions to cook it:

1. Preheat your Omni Toaster Oven to 385 degrees F in Air Fry mode
2. Take your Toaster Oven cooking basket and cover with parchment paper
3. Put tomatoes and drizzle olive oil, season with salt and cayenne
4. Transfer to your Fryer and cook for 10-15 minutes until starting to split
5. Add quartered avocado, parsley, sliced green onion, garlic, spring water, lemon juice, 1/2 teaspoon salt to a food processor
6. Blend until creamy
7. Cut zucchini ends using use spiralizer to turn into zoodles
8. Mix zoodles with sauce
9. Divide into 3 bowls and serve with tomatoes
10. Enjoy!

Nutritional value per serving:

Calories: 180 kcal, Protein: 2g, Fat: 14g, Carbs: 14g

Morning Candied Walnut And Strawberry

Looking for a crunchy way to start the day? This crunchy mix of walnut and strawberry is all that need!

Prep time and cooking time: 20 minutes | Serves: 4

Ingredients To Use:

- 1/2 cup walnuts, chopped
- 1 tablespoon raw agave nectar
- 1/4 teaspoon salt

Dressing

- 1/2 cup strawberries, sliced
- 2 tablespoons shallots
- 1/2 cup grapeseed oil
- 2 teaspoons raw agave nectar
- 1 teaspoon onion powder
- 1 and 1/2 teaspoon lime juice
- 1/2 teaspoon ginger
- 1/4 teaspoon dill
- 1/4 teaspoon salt

Step-by-Step Directions to cook it:

1. Coat walnuts with agave and salt
2. Transfer to a cooking basket lined with parchment
3. Preheat your Omni Toaster Oven to 300 degrees F in Air Fry mode, roast for 6-8 minutes
4. Let them cool
5. Add dressing ingredients to a bowl, blend for half a minute
6. Add walnuts
7. Mix and enjoy!

Nutritional value per serving:

Calories: 260 kcal, Protein: 4g, Fat: 16g, Carbs: 28g

Blueberry Pancake

Who doesn't love a good dose of pancake, right? Just go ahead and fire up your appliance in the morning to prepare this awesome delight!

Prep time and cooking time: 20 minutes | Serves: 4

Ingredients To Use:

- 2 cups all-purpose flour
- 1 cup hemp milk
- 1/2 cup spring water
- 2 tablespoons grapeseed
- 1/2 cup Agave
- 1/2 cup blueberries
- 1/4 teaspoon Sea Moss
- 2 tablespoons Hemp Seeds
- Grapeseed oil

Step-by-Step Directions to cook it:

1. Place Moss, agave, hemp seeds, grapeseed oil, flour in a large bowl
2. Mix well
3. Add milk and water, mix until you have your desired consistency
4. Toss in blueberries and toss well
5. Preheat your Omni Toaster Oven to 325 degrees F in Air Fry mode
6. Transfer batter to Toaster Oven basket lined with parchment paper
7. Cook for 3-4 minutes, flip and cook for 3 minutes more until golden on both side
8. Serve and enjoy!

Nutritional value per serving:

Calories: 279 kcal, Protein: 9g, Fat: 11g, Carbs: 36g

Masala And Quinoa Oatmeal

Tired of the boring old Quinoa and want to try out something new and spicy? This Masala Quinoa is the right dish for you!

Prep time and cooking time: 50 minutes | Serves: 4

Ingredients To Use:

- 1/2 white onion, chopped
- Pinch of salt
- 1 red bell pepper, chopped
- 1/2 jalapeno pepper, seeded and chopped
- 1 tablespoon masala powder
- 2 tablespoons ginger, peeled and grated
- 1 cup quinoa
- 2 cups Sebi friendly vegetable stock
- 1/2 lemon, juiced

Step-by-Step Directions to cook it:

1. Preheat your Omni Toaster Oven to 350 degrees F in Air Fry mode
2. Take a large skillet and place it over medium heat, add onion and salt, Sauté for 3 minutes
3. Add pepper, jalapeno, ginger, garam masala and Sauté for 1 minute
4. Add quinoa to the stock, stir
5. Transfer mix to Toaster Oven cooking basket
6. Cook for about 3-40 minutes until fluffy
7. Add lemon juice and fluff more
8. Adjust the seasoning accordingly and serve
9. Enjoy!

Nutritional value per serving:

Calories: 503 kcal, Protein: 32g, Fat: 3g, Carbs: 10g

Toasty Quinoa Chunky Bites

A walnut packed quinoa cookie, the perfect way to start off your day! Or pack in the sack for your gym-time snack.

Prep time and cooking time: 30 minutes | Serves: 4

Ingredients To Use:

- 8 ounces walnuts
- 1/2 cup uncooked quinoa
- 1 teaspoon salt
- 1 tablespoon olive oil
- 1 teaspoon ground onion powder
- 1 teaspoon paprika powder

Step-by-Step Directions to cook it:

1. Preheat your Omni Toaster Oven to 400 degrees F in Air Fry mode
2. Take a bowl and mix everything
3. Transfer mixture to Toaster Oven cooking basket lined with parchment paper
4. Bake for 10 minutes
5. Break into pieces and serve
6. Enjoy!

Nutritional value per serving:

Calories: 180 kcal, Protein: 5g, Fat: 3g, Carbs: 6g

Mexican Quinoa Lime

This Quinoa dish brings the authentic flavor of Mexico into the table! Go ahead and enjoy it!

Prep time and cooking time: 40 minutes | Serves: 4

Ingredients To Use:

- 2 tablespoons avocado oil
- 1/4 white onion, chopped
- Pinch of salt
- 2 garlic cloves, minced
- 1 cup quinoa
- 1/2 lime, juiced
- 1 tablespoon onion powder
- 1 teaspoon chili powder
- 1/4 teaspoon paprika
- 2 cups vegetable stock

Step-by-Step Directions to cook it:

1. Preheat your Omni Toaster Oven to 300 degrees F in Air Fry mode
2. Take a pan and place it over medium heat
3. Add onion and salt, Sauté for 3 minutes
4. Add garlic, quinoa, lime, cumin, chili, paprika and Sauté for 2 minutes
5. Transfer mix to Toaster Oven cooking basket
6. Add stock and cook for 20-25 minutes
7. Serve and enjoy!

Nutritional value per serving:

Calories: 266 kcal, Protein: 9g, Fat: 8g, Carbs: 8g

Quinoa And Squash Platter

If you want to try something unique and healthy, packed with flavors, this quinoa and squash are just what you need!
Prep time and cooking time: 30 minutes | Serves: 4

Ingredients To Use:

- 1 teaspoon ginger, minced
- 2 teaspoons thyme
- 1 and 1/2 cups quinoa
- 1/4 cup walnuts, chopped
- 2 onions, sliced
- 1 red bell pepper
- 2 tablespoons olive oil
- 1 big spaghetti squash
- Salt and pepper to taste

Step-by-Step Directions to cook it:

1. Preheat your Toaster Oven to 380 degrees F in Air Fry mode
2. Clean squash, slice in half
3. Transfer to Toaster Oven cooking basket and cook for 30-40 minutes until tender
4. Take a skillet and heat a tablespoon oil, add bell pepper, quinoa, onion, walnuts and cook until warm
5. Season well with salt and pepper
6. Divide mixture between squash and bake for 2-5 minutes more
7. Serve and enjoy!

Nutritional value per serving:

Calories: 428 kcal, Protein: 13g, Fat: 22g, Carbs: 49g

Original German Pancakes

Why always settle for the traditional pancake when you give it a taste and experience how the Germans make it? Give it a try, it just might be your next favorite one!

Prep time and cooking time: 30 minutes | Serves: 4

Ingredients To Use:

- 2 tablespoons apple sauce
- 1 cup flour
- 2 tablespoons maple syrup
- 3 whole eggs
- 1 cup almond milk

Step-by-Step Directions to cook it:

1. The whole ingredients should be mixed in a bowl, and the consistency of the mixture should be maintained.
2. The Omni toaster oven should be preheated at 390 F for 5 min.
3. The cast iron tray should be placed inside the air fryer.
4. The batter should be poured in the tray. The cakes are heated for 8-minute cakes are removed from the tray and served.

Nutritional value per serving:

Calories: 139 kcal, Protein: 8g, Fat: 4g, Carbs: 18g

Chapter 3: Beef, Lamb, And Pork

Macadamia Lamb Meal

Who doesn't like a lamb, right? This recipe will simply make you fall in love with them thanks to the crusty exterior and tender interior. Prep time and cooking time: 40 minutes | Serves: 4

Ingredients To Use:

- 1 garlic clove
- 1 tablespoon of olive oil
- 1 and 1/4 pound rack of lamb
- Pepper as required
- Salt as required

For Macadamia Crust

- 3-ounce unsalted macadamia nuts
- 1 tablespoon of breadcrumbs
- 1 tablespoon of freshly chopped rosemary
- 1 egg

Step-by-Step Directions to cook it:

1. Chop up the garlic and add them to olive oil and mix well to prepare your garlic oil
2. Take your lamb rack and brush it with the prepared oil
3. Season the rack with pepper and salt
4. Preheat your Omni Toaster Oven to the temperature of 220 degrees Fahrenheit in Air Fry mode

5. Take a bowl and add the ingredients under the Macadamia crust
6. Take another bowl and beat the eggs and whisk them well
7. Dip your meat in the egg mix and drain excess
8. Coat the lamb rack with the macadamia crust mixture
9. Place the rack in your cooking basket
10. Cook for about 30 minutes
11. Increase the temperature of the Toaster Oven to 390 degrees Fahrenheit after 30 minutes and cook for 5 minutes more
12. Remove the meat and allow them to cool
13. Cover the meat with aluminum foil and allow them to cool for 10 minutes
14. Enjoy!

Nutritional value per serving:

Calories: 327 kcal, Protein: 47g, Fat: 70g, Carbs: 0g

Honey-Licious Pork Dish

You really just can't go wrong with pork dredged in delicious honey.
Prep time and cooking time: 30 minutes | Serves: 4

Ingredients To Use:

- 1 pound pork ribs
- 1 teaspoon salt
- 1 teaspoon pepper
- 1 tablespoon sugar
- 1 teaspoon ginger Juice
- 1 teaspoon five-spice powder
- 1 tablespoon teriyaki sauce
- 1 tablespoon light soy sauce
- 1 garlic cloves, minced
- 2 tablespoon honey
- 1 tablespoon water
- 1 tablespoon tomato sauce

Step-by-Step Directions to cook it:

1. Take a bowl and add pepper, sugar, salt, five-spice powder, teriyaki sauce, and ginger sauce to prepare the marinade
2. Season the pork ribs with the mixture
3. Allow it to marinate for about 2 hours
4. Pre-heat your Omni Toaster Oven to a temperature of 350 degrees Fahrenheit in Air Fry mode
5. Place the pork ribs in the Omni Toaster Oven cooking basket and cook for about 8 minutes
6. Take another mixing bowl and add soy sauce, garlic, honey, water, and tomato sauce
7. Mix well

8. Take a skillet and place it over medium heat
9. Add some oil and stir fry garlic until they release a nice fragrance
10. Add your fried pork ribs to the skillet alongside the prepared sauce and stir fry until it is fully coated with the sauce
11. Serve and enjoy!

Nutritional value per serving:

Calories: 186 kcal, Protein: 15g, Fat: 11g, Carbs: 5g

Lamb Chop Raita

Ever thought why Indian Lamb's taste so well? The secret sauce is the "Raita," and this is how you prepare your lamb with raita.

Prep time and cooking time: 20 minutes | Serves: 4

Ingredients To Use:

- 4 tablespoon of natural low-fat yogurt
- 1 teaspoon of cumin seeds
- 1 tablespoon of crushed coriander seed
- 1/2 a spoon of chili powder
- 2 teaspoon of Garam masala
- 2 tablespoon of lime juice
- 1 teaspoon of salt
- 4 lamb chops
- Raita

Step-by-Step Directions to cook it:

1. Take your lamb chops and coat them with a mixture of salt, lime juice, spices and salt
2. Leave the lamb chops for about an hour
3. Pre-heat your Omni Toaster Oven to a temperature of 392 degrees Fahrenheit in Air Fry mode
4. Transfer the Lamb Chops to your frying basket and cook for 10 minutes
5. Enjoy with some rice and Raita on top!

Nutritional value per serving:

Calories: 275 kcal, Protein: 39g, Fat: 11g, Carbs: 2g

Nam Jim Beef Salad

These meatballs are simply top of the line when it comes to meatballs! A meal from the streets of Thailand, it'll make you fall in love with it.

Prep time and cooking time: 20 minutes | Serves: 4

Ingredients To Use:

Meatball Ingredients

- 16 ounce of grounded lamb
- 4 ounces of grounded beef
- 1-1/2 tablespoon of finely chopped parsley
- 1 teaspoon of grounded cumin
- 1 teaspoon of grounded coriander
- 1 teaspoon of cayenne pepper
- 1 teaspoon of red chili paste
- 2 cloves of finely chopped garlic
- 1/4 cup of olive oil
- 1 teaspoon of salt
- 1 egg white

For the Mint Yogurt, you will need

- 1/2 a cup of non-fat Greek yogurt
- 1/4 cup of sour cream
- 2 tablespoons of buttermilk
- 1/4 cup of finely chopped mint
- 1 clove of finely chopped garlic
- 2 pinches of salt

Step-by-Step Directions to cook it:

1. Pre-heat your Omni Toaster Oven to a temperature of 390

degrees Fahrenheit in Air Fry mode
2. Take a large-sized bowl and add the listed ingredients for meatballs
3. Mix well and roll the mixture into balls
4. Smooth out the surface of the balls
5. Take your cooking basket and place the balls in the cooking basket
6. Allow them to cook for 8 minutes
7. Take another bowl and add the remaining ingredients under yogurt and mix them well to prepare your mint yogurt
8. Serve the cooked meatballs with the yogurt and a garnish of mint and olives

Nutritional value per serving:

Calories: 197 kcal, Protein: 7g, Fat: 4g, Carbs: 32g

Potato Herb Beef Roast

A completely herbed up beef roast with some added potatoes, yum!
Prep time and cooking time: 20 minutes | Serves: 4

Ingredients To Use:

- 2 teaspoon of olive oil
- 4 pound of top round roast beef
- 1 teaspoon of salt
- 1/4 teaspoon of fresh ground black pepper
- 1 teaspoon of dried thyme
- 1/2 a teaspoon of finely chopped fresh rosemary
- 3 pound of halved red potatoes
- Olive oil freshly ground black pepper and salt

Step-by-Step Directions to cook it:

1. Preheat your Omni Toaster Oven to a temperature of 360 degrees Fahrenheit in Air Fry mode
2. Rub olive oil all over the beef
3. Take a bowl and add salt, thyme, pepper, rosemary and mix well
4. Season the beef with this mixture
5. Transfer the seasoned mix into Omni Toaster Oven and cook for 20 minutes
6. Add potatoes with some oil and pepper
7. Turn the roast over and add the potatoes into the cooking basket
8. Cook for 20 minutes more
9. Make sure to rotate the roast for a few times
10. Cook until you have reached your desired temperature (130F for Rare, 140F for Medium and 160F for Well Done)
11. Allow it to cool for 5-10 minutes

12. Pre-heat your Omni Toaster Oven temperature to 400 degrees Fahrenheit and keep cooking the potatoes for 8-10 minutes are browned

13. Shake and serve with the beef!

Nutritional value per serving:

Calories: 514 kcal, Protein: 39g, Fat: 37g, Carbs: 5g

Beef Broccoli Delight

Want to eat broccoli but think that they are not yummy enough?
This beef broccoli meal is what you need!
Prep time and cooking time: 30 minutes | Serves: 4

- 3/4 pound of circular beef steak cut up into thin strips
- 1 pound of broccoli with stems removed and cut up into florets
- 1/3 cup of oyster sauce
- 2 teaspoon of sesame oil
- 1/3 cup of sherry
- 1 teaspoon of soy sauce
- 1 teaspoon of white sugar
- 1 teaspoon of cornstarch
- 1 tablespoon of olive oil
- 1 freshly sliced ginger root
- 1 garlic clove, minced

Step-by-Step Directions to cook it:

1. Take a small-sized bowl and add oyster sauce, cornstarch, sesame oil, sherry, sugar, and soy sauce
2. Add the steak strips and marinate for 45 minutes
3. Pre-heat your Omni Toaster Oven to 390 degrees F in Air Fry mode
4. Once the steak is ready, add them to the Toaster Oven cooking basket alongside broccoli
5. Add garlic, olive oil and ginger
6. Cook for about 12 minutes at 390 degrees Fahrenheit
7. Serve over rice
8. Enjoy!

Nutritional value per serving:

Calories: 350 kcal, Protein: 20g, Fat: 18g, Carbs: 50g

Mouthwatering Mushroom Pork Chops

Mushroom and Pork Chops are just a match made in heaven!
Prep time and cooking time: 50 minutes | Serves: 4

Ingredients To Use:

- 8 ounces mushrooms, sliced
- 1 teaspoon garlic
- 1 onion, peeled and chopped
- 1 cup Keto-Friendly Mayonnaise
- 3 pork chops, boneless
- 1 teaspoon ground nutmeg
- 1 tablespoon balsamic vinegar
- 1/2 cup of coconut oil

Step-by-Step Directions to cook it:

1. Take a pan and place it over medium heat
2. Add oil and let it heat up
3. Add mushrooms, onions, and stir
4. Cook for 4 minutes
5. Add pork chops, season with nutmeg, garlic powder, and brown both sides
6. Transfer the pan in the Toaster Oven and bake for 30 minutes at 350 degrees F in Bake Mode
7. Transfer pork chops to plates and keep it warm
8. Take a pan and place it over medium heat
9. Add vinegar, mayonnaise over mushroom mix and stir or a few minutes
10. Drizzle sauce over pork chops
11. Enjoy!

Nutritional value per serving:

Calories: 600 kcal, Protein: 30g, Fat: 10g, Carbs: 8g

Herby Butter Pork Chops

Looking for juicy, delicious pork dripping with butter and Italian herbs? Jump right in!

Prep time and cooking time: 30 minutes | Serves: 4

Ingredients To Use:

- 1 tablespoon butter, divided
- 2 boneless pork chops
- Salt and pepper to taste
- 1 tablespoon dried Italian seasoning
- 1 tablespoon olive oil

Step-by-Step Directions to cook it:

1. Preheat your Omni Toaster Oven to 350 degrees F in Bake Mode
2. Pat pork chops dry with a paper towel and place them in a baking dish
3. Season with salt, pepper, and Italian seasoning
4. Drizzle olive oil over pork chops
5. Top each chop with 1/2 tablespoon butter
6. Bake for 25 minutes
7. Transfer pork chops on two plates and top with butter juice
8. Serve and enjoy!

Nutritional value per serving:

Calories: 333 kcal, Protein: 31g, Fat: 23g, Carbs: 1g

Beef And Tomato Squash

Beef mixed with Acorn Squash and mushrooms, the dish will just melt in your mouth!

Prep time and cooking time: 70 minutes | Serves: 4

Ingredients To Use:

- 2 pounds acorn squash, pricked with a fork
- Salt and pepper to taste
- 3 garlic cloves, peeled and minced
- 1 onion, peeled and chopped
- 1 portobello mushroom, sliced
- 28 ounces canned tomatoes, diced
- 1 teaspoon dried oregano
- 1/4 teaspoon cayenne pepper
- 1/2 teaspoon dried thyme
- 1 pound ground beef
- 1 green bell pepper, seeded and chopped

Step-by-Step Directions to cook it:

1. Pre-heat your Toaster Oven to 400 degrees F in Bake Mode
2. Take acorn squash and transfer to the lined baking sheet, bake for 40 minutes
3. Cut in half and let it cool
4. Deseed them
5. Take a pan and place it over medium-high heat, add meat, garlic, onion, and mushroom, stir cook until brown
6. Add salt, pepper, thyme, oregano, cayenne, tomatoes, green pepper, and stir
7. Cook for 10 minutes
8. Stuff squash halves with beef mix

9. Transfer to Toaster Oven and bake for 10 minutes more
10. Serve and enjoy!

Nutritional value per serving:

Calories: 200 kcal, Protein: 10g, Fat: 7g, Carbs: 4g

Smothered Pork Chop Delight

Looking for something simple yet elegant? These smothered bone-in chops are exactly what you need!

Prep time and cooking time: 40 minutes | Serves: 4

Ingredients To Use:

- 4 pork chops, bone-in
- 2 tablespoon of olive oil
- 1/4 cup of vegetable broth
- 1/2 a pound of Yukon gold potatoes, peeled and chopped
- 1 large onion, sliced
- 2 garlic cloves, minced
- 2 teaspoon of rubbed sage
- 1 teaspoon of thyme, ground
- Pepper as needed

Step-by-Step Directions to cook it:

1. Pre-heat your Toaster Oven to 350 degrees Fahrenheit in Bake Mode
2. Take a large-sized skillet and place it over medium heat
3. Add a tablespoon of oil and allow the oil to heat up
4. Add pork chops and cook them for 4-5 minutes per side until browned
5. Transfer chops to a baking dish
6. Pour broth over the chops
7. Add remaining oil to the pan and Saute potatoes, onion, garlic for 3-4 minutes
8. Take a large bowl and add potatoes, garlic, onion, thyme, sage, pepper
9. Transfer this mixture to the baking dish (with pork)
10. Bake for 20-30 minutes
11. Serve and enjoy!

Nutritional value per serving:

Calories: 37 kcal, Protein: 1g, Fat: 3g, Carbs: 2g

Chapter 4: Chicken And Poultry Recipes

Spicy Jamaican Jerk Chicken

Want something spicy and breathtaking? These Jamaican Jerk chicken are the way to go!

Prep time and cooking time: 30 minutes | Serves: 4

Ingredients To Use:

- 48 ounce of chicken wings
- 2 tablespoon of olive oil
- 2 tablespoons of soy sauce
- 6 cloves of finely chopped garlic
- 1 piece of the finely chopped habanero pepper with its seeds and ribs removed.
- 1 tablespoon of allspice
- 1 tablespoon of cinnamon
- 1 tablespoon of cayenne pepper
- 1 tablespoon of White pepper
- 1 tablespoon of salt
- 2 tablespoons of brown sugar
- 1 tablespoon of finely chopped up fresh thyme
- 1 tablespoon of freshly grated ginger
- 4 finely chopped up scallion
- 5 tablespoons of lemon juice
- 1/2 a cup of wine vinegar

Step-by-Step Directions to cook it:

1. Take a large-sized mixing bowl and add the ingredients (except chicken) and mix well to prepare the seasoning
2. Take a 1 gallon-sized resealable bag and add the chicken wings and seasoning and give it a shake to ensure that the chickens are coated up
3. Allow it to marinate for about 2 hours to 24 hours
4. Pre-heat your Omni Toaster Oven to a temperature of 390 degrees Fahrenheit in Air Fry mode
5. Take the wings off the bag and drain the excess liquid
6. Take a paper towel and pat the wings dry
7. Place them on your cooking basket and cook for about 16-18 minutes
8. Shake the basket about halfway through
9. Serve the chickens with some blue cheese or ranch dressing
10. Enjoy!

Nutritional value per serving:

Calories: 20 kcal, Protein: 1g, Fat: 0g, Carbs: 20g

Juicy Korean Chicken

Korean dishes are already known for their awesome and unique flavors, why not make one at home and try out why they are so cool? Prep time and cooking time: 30 minutes | Serves: 4

Ingredients To Use:

- 1 pound of chicken wings
- 8 ounce of flour
- 8 ounce of bread crumbs
- 3 beaten eggs
- 4 tablespoon Canola oil
- Salt as needed
- Pepper as needed
- 2 teaspoon of sesame seeds
- 2 tablespoon of Korean red pepper paste
- 1 tablespoon of apple cider vinegar
- 1 tablespoon of hot water
- 2 tablespoon of honey
- 1 tablespoon of soy sauce

Step-by-Step Directions to cook it:

1. Separate the chicken wings into winglets and drumlets
2. Take a bowl and add salt, oil, pepper
3. Season, the chicken with the mixture
4. Preheat your Omni Instant Fryer Oven to a temperature of 350 degrees Fahrenheit in Air Fry mode
5. Take a bowl and add flour, beaten eggs, and bread crumbs
6. Mix well
7. Dredge the chicken wings into the mixture and transfer them to your Toaster Oven cooking basket

8. Cook for 15 minutes
9. Take a saucepan and add red pepper paste, apple cider vinegar, water, soy sauce, and honey
10. Mix well
11. Bring the whole mixture to a boil
12. Transfer your cooked chicken to this mixture and stir well to ensure that the chicken is coated well
13. Garnish the chicken with some sesame and enjoy it!

Nutritional value per serving:

Calories: 250 kcal, Protein: 13g, Fat: 9g, Carbs: 12g

Cheesy Chicken Meal

Cheese lover? This chicken dish is the meal for you!
Prep time and cooking time: 20 minutes | Serves: 4

Ingredients To Use:

- 2 pieces of 8 ounces chicken breast with the fat trimmed and sliced up in half (making 4 portions)
- 6 tablespoon of seasoned breadcrumbs
- 2 tablespoon of grated parmesan
- 1 tablespoon of melted butter
- Tablespoon of low-fat mozzarella cheese
- 1/2 a cup of marinara sauce
- Cooking spray as needed

Step-by-Step Directions to cook it:

1. Pre-heat your Omni Toaster Oven to 390 degrees Fahrenheit for about 9 minutes in Air Fry mode
2. Take the cooking basket and spray it evenly with cooking spray
3. Take a small bowl and add breadcrumbs and parmesan cheese
4. Mix them well
5. Take another bowl and add the butter, melt it in your microwave
6. Brush the chicken pieces with the butter and dredge them into the breadcrumb mix
7. Once the fryer is ready, place 2 pieces of your prepared chicken breast and spray the top a bit of oil
8. Cook for about 6 minutes
9. Turn them over and top them up with 1 tablespoon of Marinara and 1 and a 1/2 tablespoon of shredded mozzarella

10. Cook for 3 minutes more until the cheese has completely melted
11. Keep the cooked breasts on the side and repeat with the remaining pieces

Nutritional value per serving:

Calories: 251 kcal, Protein: 31g, Fat: 10g, Carbs: 14g

Fully Crusted Up Chicken Escallops

These chicken escallops are simply to die for! The exterior crust is just a bonus!

Prep time and cooking time: 60 minutes | Serves: 4

- 4 skinless chicken breast
- 2 and a 1/2 ounce of panko breadcrumbs
- 1 ounce of grated parmesan
- 6 pieces of finely chopped sage leaves
- 1 and a 3/4 ounce of plain flour
- 2 beaten eggs

1. Place the chicken between cling film and beat it roughly using a rolling pin to and give it a thickness of 1/2 cm
2. Take a bowl and add parmesan, sage, and breadcrumbs
3. Take another bowl and add flour and season with salt
4. Dredge the chicken in the seasoned flour followed by dredging them in the beaten egg and finally in the bread crumbs mix
5. Pre-heat your Omni Toaster Oven to a temperature of 392 degrees Fahrenheit in Air Fry mode
6. Take your cooking basket and spray it well
7. Spray the chicken with some oil as well
8. Place two of the pieces at a time in your cooking basket and cook for 4 minutes until a golden texture is seen
9. Once done, serve with a green salad
10. Enjoy!

Calories: 363 kcal, Protein: 50g, Fat: 5g, Carbs: 35g

Korean BBQ Satay

Yet another Korean dish to die for! The famous street food of Korean Satay is here for your amazing Omni Plus!
Prep time and cooking time: 20 minutes | Serves: 4

Ingredients To Use:

- 3/4rth ounces of boneless and skinless chicken tenders
- 1/2 cup of low sodium soy sauce
- 1/2 cup of pineapple juice
- 1/4th cup of sesame oil
- 4 cloves of chopped up garlic
- 4 chopped up scallions
- 1 tablespoon of freshly grated ginger
- 2 teaspoon of toasted sesame seeds
- 1 pinch of black pepper

Step-by-Step Directions to cook it:

1. Skewer the chicken pieces into the skewers and trim down any excess fat
2. Take a large bowl and add the remaining ingredients
3. Dip the skewered chicken into the bowl
4. Allow them to marinate for about 2-24 hours
5. Preheat your Toaster Oven to 390 degrees Fahrenheit in Air Fry mode
6. Remove the chicken and place it on a towel to dry
7. Place them on your cooking basket and cook for 5-7 minutes
8. Enjoy!

Nutritional value per serving:

Calories: 361 kcal, Protein: 26g, Fat: 12g, Carbs: 37g

Pickled Salty Chicken

Who said pickled meals have to be hard to swallow? These chicken are simply irresistible!

Prep time and cooking time: 50 minutes | Serves: 4

Ingredients To Use:

- 4 pieces of chicken legs cut up into drumsticks and thigh
- Pickle juice from 25-ounce kosher dill pickle jar
- 1/2 a cup of flour
- Salt as needed
- Ground black pepper as needed
- 2 pieces of beaten eggs
- 2 tablespoon of vegetable oil
- 1 cup of fine breadcrumbs
- 1 teaspoon of salt
- 1 teaspoon of freshly ground black pepper
- 1/2 a teaspoon of ground paprika
- 1/8 teaspoon of cayenne pepper
- Vegetable oil for spraying

Step-by-Step Directions to cook it:

1. Take a shallow dish and add chicken
2. Pour pickle juice and allow your chicken to brine for 3-8 hours in your fridge (covered)
3. Remove and allow it to come to room temperature
4. Take three bowls and add seasoned flour, whisked egg and veggie oil, and a mixture of breadcrumbs, salt, pepper, paprika, and cayenne pepper into the third bowl
5. Pre-heat your Omni Toaster Oven to a temperature of 370 degrees Fahrenheit in Air Fry mode

6. Remove the chicken from pickle brine and dry them with a kitchen towel
7. Dredge them in the flour, egg, and breadcrumb
8. Spray with some vegetable oil
9. Cook the chickens in batches, cook the first batch for 10 minutes making sure to them once done
10. Cook for 10 minutes more
11. Repeat with the second batch
12. Lower your temperature of 340 degrees Fahrenheit
13. Place the first batch of chicken on top of the second batch (already in the fryer)
14. Fry for 7 minutes more
15. Enjoy!

Nutritional value per serving:

Calories: 246 kcal, Protein: 30g, Fat: 12g, Carbs: 2g

Hearty Indian Chicken Tikka

The classical Indian Chicken Tikka! You just can't go wrong with this.

Prep time and cooking time: 20 minutes | Serves: 4

Ingredients To Use:

- 17 ounce of boneless chicken cut up into small portions
- 7 ounce of thick yogurt
- Three colored bell peppers cut up into inch chunks
- 3 and a 1/2 ounce of cherry tomatoes
- 1 tablespoon of fresh ginger garlic paste
- 2 tablespoon of red Chili powder
- 1 teaspoon of Turmeric powder
- 2 tablespoon of Coriander powder
- 2 tablespoon of Cumin powder
- 2 teaspoon of Olive oil
- Salt as needed
- Pepper as needed

For Garnish

- 1/3 cup of chopped fresh coriander
- Few mint leaves
- 1 thinly sliced onion
- 1 lemon cut in half

Step-by-Step Directions to cook it:

1. Take a large-sized bowl and add all of the ingredients under marinade and add the chicken with spices
2. Coat well and allow it to sit for 2 hours
3. Thread the chicken, tomatoes, and peppers alternatively into skewers and keep them on the side

4. Pre-heat your Omni Toaster Oven to 390 degrees Fahrenheit in Air Fry mode
5. Line up your cooking basket with aluminum foil and place the skewers
6. Grill for about 12-15 minutes
7. Remove and garnish with mint, coriander, onion and a squeeze of lime
8. Enjoy!

Nutritional value per serving:

Calories: 120 kcal, Protein: 2g, Fat: 3g, Carbs: 21g

Broody Blackened Chicken

The original Blackened Chicken recipe, now for your Omni Plus appliance! Go ahead and fire away!

Prep time and cooking time: 20 minutes | Serves: 4

Ingredients To Use:

- 1/2 teaspoon paprika
- 1/8 teaspoon salt
- 1/4 teaspoon cayenne pepper
- 1/4 teaspoon ground cumin
- 1/4 teaspoon dried thyme
- 1/8 teaspoon ground white pepper
- 1/8 teaspoon onion powder
- 2 chicken breasts, boneless and skinless

Step-by-Step Directions to cook it:

1. Pre-heat your Omni Toaster Oven to 350-degree Fahrenheit in bake mode
2. Grease baking sheet
3. Take a cast-iron skillet and place it over high heat
4. Add oil and heat it for 5 minutes until smoking hot
5. Take a small bowl and mix salt, paprika, cumin, white pepper, cayenne, thyme, onion powder
6. Oil the chicken breast on both sides and coat the breast with the spice mix
7. Transfer to your hot pan and cook for 1 minute per side
8. Transfer to your prepared baking sheet and bake for 5 minutes
9. Serve and enjoy!

Nutritional value per serving:

Calories: 150 kcal, Protein: 24g, Fat: 3g, Carbs: 1g

Exquisite Almond Butternut Chicken

Want to ante up the health factor of your chicken meal? Prepare it with some butternut squash, and you are good to go!

Prep time and cooking time: 45 minutes | Serves: 4

Ingredients To Use:

- 1/2 pound Nitrate free bacon
- Extra virgin olive oil
- 6 chicken thighs, boneless and skinless
- 2-3 cups almond butternut squash, cubed
- Fresh chopped sage
- Sunflower seeds and pepper as needed

Step-by-Step Directions to cook it:

1. Prepare your Omni Toaster Oven by preheating it to 425 degrees F in Bake Mode
2. Take a large skillet and place it over medium-high heat, add bacon and fry until crispy
3. Take bacon and place it on the side, crumbled the bacon
4. Add cubed almond butternut squash in the bacon grease and Sauté, season with sunflower seeds and pepper
5. Once the squash is tender, remove skillet and transfer to a plate
6. Add coconut oil to the skillet and add chicken thigh, cook for 10 minutes
7. Season with sunflower seeds and pepper
8. Remove skillet from the stove and transfer to Toaster Oven
9. Bake for 12-15 minutes, top with crumbled bacon and sage
10. Enjoy!

Nutritional value per serving:

Calories: 136 kcal, Protein: 24g, Fat: 3g, Carbs: 1g

Lemon And Pepper Chicken

Simple and efficient Lemon And Pepper chicken, the perfect balance of tangy and heat, perfect lunch for busy any day!
Prep time and cooking time: 20 minutes | Serves: 4

- 2 teaspoons olive oil
- 1 and 1/4 pounds skinless chicken cutlets
- 2 whole eggs
- 1/4 cup panko
- 1 tablespoon lemon pepper
- Sunflower seeds and pepper to taste
- 3 cups green beans
- 1/4 cup parmesan cheese
- 1/4 teaspoon garlic powder

Step-by-Step Directions to cook it:

1. Pre-heat your Omni Toaster Oven to 425 degrees F in Bake Mode
2. Take a bowl and stir in seasoning, parmesan, lemon pepper, garlic powder, panko
3. Whisk eggs in another bowl
4. Coat cutlets in eggs and press into panko mix
5. Transfer coated chicken to a parchment-lined a baking sheet
6. Toss the beans in oil, pepper, and sunflower seeds, lay them on the side of the baking sheet
7. Bake for 15 minutes
8. Enjoy!

Nutritional value per serving:

Calories: 136 kcal, Protein: 24g, Fat: 3g, Carbs: 1g

Chapter 5: Fish And Seafood Recipes

Walnut Crusted Salmon

Looking for a fish meal but want it to be a bit more crunchy? This Crunchy Salmon meal is the one to go with!

Prep time and cooking time: 30 minutes | Serves: 4

Ingredients To Use:

- 1/2 cup walnuts
- 2 tablespoons stevia
- 1/2 tablespoon Dijon mustard
- 1/4 teaspoon dill
- 2 Salmon fillets (3 ounces each)
- 1 tablespoon olive oil
- Sunflower seeds and pepper to taste

Step-by-Step Directions to cook it:

1. Preheat your Omni toaster oven to 350 degrees F in bake mode
2. Add walnuts, mustard, stevia to a food processor and process until your desired consistency is achieved
3. Take a frying pan and place it over medium heat
4. Add oil and let it heat up
5. Add salmon and sear for 3 minutes
6. Add walnut mix and coat well
7. Transfer coated salmon to the baking sheet, bake in the oven for 8 minutes
8. Serve and enjoy!

Nutritional value per serving:

Calories: 373 kcal, Protein: 20g, Fat: 43g, Carbs: 4g

Pistachio Sole Fish

Who says sole fish should be left alone? Add a bit of pistachio, and they will turn into one of the most delish dishes out there!
Prep time and cooking time: 20 minutes | Serves: 4

Ingredients To Use:

- 4 (5 ounces) boneless sole fillets
- Sunflower seeds and pepper as needed
- 1/2 cup pistachios, finely chopped
- Juice of 1 lemon
- 1 teaspoon extra virgin olive oil

Step-by-Step Directions to cook it:

1. Preheat your Omni toaster oven to 350 degrees Fahrenheit in Bake Mode
2. Line a baking sheet with parchment paper and keep it on the side
3. Pat fish dry with kitchen towels and lightly season with sunflower seeds and pepper
4. Take a small bowl and stir in pistachios
5. Place sol on the prepped sheet and press 2 tablespoons of pistachio mixture on top of each fillet
6. Drizzle fish with lemon juice and olive oil
7. Bake for 10 minutes until the top is golden and fish flakes with a fork
8. Serve and enjoy!

Nutritional value per serving:

Calories: 166 kcal, Protein: 26g, Fat: 6g, Carbs: 2g

Tilapia Broccoli Meal

Add a bit of broccoli to your tilapia dish to improve not only the flavors but also the health factor!

Prep time and cooking time: 20 minutes | Serves: 4

Ingredients To Use:

- 6 ounce of tilapia, frozen
- 1 tablespoon almond butter
- 1 tablespoon of garlic, minced
- 1 teaspoon of lemon pepper seasoning
- 1 cup of broccoli florets, fresh

Step-by-Step Directions to cook it:

1. Pre-heat your Toaster Oven to 350 degrees F in bake mode
2. Add fish in aluminum foil packets
3. Arrange broccoli around fish
4. Sprinkle lemon pepper on top
5. Close the packets and seal
6. Bake for 14 minutes
7. Take a bowl and add garlic and butter, mix well and keep the mixture on the side
8. Remove the packet from Toaster Oven and transfer to a platter
9. Place butter on top of the fish and broccoli, serve and enjoy!

Nutritional value per serving:

Calories: 362 kcal, Protein: 29g, Fat: 25g, Carbs: 2g

Asparagus And Lemon Salmon

Authentic Lemon flavored Salmon Dish, mixed with a buck load of citric flavor to give a nice kick!

Prep time and cooking time: 30 minutes | Serves: 4

Ingredients To Use:

- 2 salmon fillets, 6 ounces each, skin on
- Salt to taste
- 1 pound asparagus, trimmed
- 2 cloves garlic, minced
- 3 tablespoons almond butter
- 1/4 cup cashew cheese

Step-by-Step Directions to cook it:

1. Pre-heat your Omni Toaster Oven to 400 degrees F in bake mode
2. Line a baking sheet with oil
3. Take a kitchen towel and pat your salmon dry, season as needed
4. Put salmon around the baking sheet and arrange asparagus around it
5. Place a pan over medium heat and melt butter
6. Add garlic and cook for 3 minutes until garlic browns slightly
7. Drizzle sauce over salmon
8. Sprinkle salmon with parmesan and bake for 12 minutes until salmon looks cooked all the way and is flaky
9. Serve and enjoy!

Nutritional value per serving:

Calories: 434 kcal, Protein: 42g, Fat: 26g, Carbs: 6g

Garlic And Butter Shrimp

Who doesn't like butter, right? And who doesn't love shrimp? Add both of them together, and you have a dish that is one for the ages! Prep time and cooking time: 45 minutes | Serves: 4

Ingredients To Use:

- 4 pounds shrimp
- 1-2 tablespoons garlic, minced
- 1/2 cup almond butter
- 1 tablespoon lemon pepper seasoning
- 1/2 teaspoon garlic powder

Step-by-Step Directions to cook it:

1. Pre-heat your Omni Toaster Oven to 300-degree F in bake mode
2. Take a bowl and mix in garlic and butter
3. Place shrimp in a pan and dot with butter garlic mix
4. Sprinkle garlic powder and lemon pepper
5. Bake for 30 minutes
6. Enjoy!

Nutritional value per serving:

Calories: 749 kcal, Protein: 74g, Fat: 30g, Carbs: 7g

Spiced Up Roasted Shrimp Meal

Looking for a shrimp dish that packs a spicy punch? This is the dish for you!

Prep time and cooking time: 20 minutes | Serves: 4

Ingredients To Use:

- 1/2 ounces large shrimp, peeled and deveined
- Cooking spray as needed
- 1 teaspoon low sodium coconut aminos
- 1 teaspoon parsley
- 1/2 teaspoon olive oil
- 1/2 tablespoon honey
- 1 tablespoon lemon juice

Step-by-Step Directions to cook it:

1. Pre-heat your Omni Toaster Oven to 450 degrees F in Toast Mode
2. Take a baking dish and grease it well
3. Mix in all the ingredients and toss
4. Transfer to Toaster Oven and bake for 8 minutes until shrimp turn pink
5. Serve and enjoy!

Nutritional value per serving:

Calories: 284 kcal, Protein: 32g, Fat: 18g, Carbs: 1g

Bacon Scallops

Do you know what's even tastier than regular scallops? Wrapping them up with bacon! Join in and fall in love with it!
Prep time and cooking time: 30 minutes | Serves: 4

Ingredients To Use:

- 1 pound bacon, uncured
- 2 pounds sea scallops, fresh and patted dry
- Lemon wedges
- 3 tablespoon golden ghee
- 1/4 cup dry white wine

Step-by-Step Directions to cook it:

1. Line two baking sheets with parchment paper
2. Pre-heat your Omni Toaster Oven to 400 degrees F in Bake Mode
3. Put bacon strips on sheet evenly, bake for 15 minutes
4. Crumbled once cooked and cooled
5. Take a skillet and place it over high heat
6. Pour the grease and heat it up
7. Brown scallops in oil, cook for 3 minutes each side
8. Set scallops on the side and add wine to the skillet
9. Use wine to deglaze the pan, scrape brown bits
10. Add ghee and make a wine sauce
11. Add scallops and bacon
12. Toss and cook for 1 minute more
13. Enjoy!

Nutritional value per serving:

Calories: 550 kcal, Protein: 66g, Fat: 27g, Carbs: 6g

Rosemary Butter Prawns

Buttery prawns with rosemary? Sign me up!
Prep time and cooking time: 20 minutes | Serves: 4

Ingredients To Use:

- 8 large prawns
- 1 rosemary sprig, chopped
- 1/2 tablespoon melted butter
- Salt and pepper to taste

Step-by-Step Directions to cook it:

1. Combine butter, rosemary, salt, and pepper in a bowl. Add in the prawns and mix to coat. Cover the bowl and refrigerate for 1 hour.
2. Preheat Omni Toaster Oven on Air Fry function to 350 F Remove the prawns from the fridge and place them in the basket.
3. Fit in the baking tray and cook for 10 minutes, flipping once. Serve.

Nutritional value per serving:

Calories: 558 kcal, Protein: 20g, Fat: 22g, Carbs: 71g

Garlic And Butter Catfish

Some people often think that Catfish isn't that delicious as some of the other brethren, such as your Salmon or Tilapia. But if you prepare this meal the way we explained it here, you'll just keep coming back for more!

Prep time and cooking time: 25 minutes | Serves: 4

Ingredients To Use:

- 2 tablespoons cilantro
- 1 garlic clove, mashed
- 2 tablespoons melted
- 1 lime juice
- 2 teaspoons blackening seasoning
- 2 catfish filets

Step-by-Step Directions to cook it:

1. In a bowl, blend in garlic, lime juice, cilantro, and butter.
2. Pour half of the mixture over the fillets and sprinkle with blackening seasoning.
3. Place the fillets in the basket and fit in the baking tray;
4. Cook for 15 minutes at 360 F on Air Fry function. Serve the fish with remaining sauce.

Nutritional value per serving:

Calories: 217 kcal, Protein: 19g, Fat: 11g, Carbs: 8g

Classic Old Bay Tilapia Fillets

Tilapia with Old Bay seasoning, a solid combination if there ever was one!

Prep time and cooking time: 20 minutes | Serves: 4

Ingredients To Use:

- 2-3 butter buds
- Salt to taste
- 2 tablespoons lemon pepper
- 2 tablespoons canola oil
- 1 tablespoon old bay seasoning
- pound tilapia fillets

Step-by-Step Directions to cook it:

1. Preheat your Omni Toaster Oven to 400 F on the Bake function. Drizzle tilapia fillets with canola oil.
2. In a bowl, mix salt, lemon pepper, butter buds, and seasoning; spread on the fish. Place the fillet on the basket and fit in the baking tray.
3. Cook for 10 minutes, flipping once until tender and crispy.

Nutritional value per serving:

Calories: 453 kcal, Protein: 39g, Fat: 22g, Carbs: 25g

Chapter 6: Vegan And Vegetarian Recipes

Kale And Chickpea Delight

Crispy chickpea bites dressed with Italian herbs, just close your eyes and go for it!

Prep time and cooking time: 40 minutes | Serves: 4

Ingredients To Use:

- 2 cups chickpea flour
- 1/2 cup green bell pepper, diced
- 1/2 cup onions, minced
- 1 tablespoon oregano
- 1 tablespoon salt
- 1 teaspoon cayenne
- 4 cups spring water
- 2 tablespoons Grape Seed Oil

Step-by-Step Directions to cook it:

1. Boil spring water in a large pot
2. Lower heat to medium and whisk in chickpea flour
3. Add minced onions, diced green bell pepper, seasoning to the pot and cook for 10 minutes
4. Cover a dish with a baking sheet, grease with oil
5. Pour batter on the sheet and spread with a spatula
6. Cover with another sheet
7. Transfer to fridge and chill for 20 minutes

8. Remove from freezer and cut batter into fry shapes
9. Preheat your Omni Toaster Oven to 385 degrees F in Air Fry mode
10. Transfer fries to the cooking basket, lightly greased and cover with parchment
11. Bake for 15 minutes, flip and bake for 10 minutes more until golden brown
12. Serve and enjoy!

Nutritional value per serving:

Calories: 271 kcal, Protein: 9g, Fat: 15, Carbs: 28g

Turmeric Nuggets

've we all had chicken nuggets, right? Then why not try out some healthy turmeric nuggets, right?

Prep time and cooking time: 40 minutes | Serves: 4

Ingredients To Use:

- 2 cups cauliflower florets
- 1 cup carrots, chopped
- 2 cups broccoli florets
- 1/2 cup almond meal
- 2 eggs, pasture-raised
- 1 teaspoon garlic, minced
- 1/2 teaspoon turmeric, grounded
- 1/4 teaspoon salt
- 1/4 teaspoon black pepper

Step-by-Step Directions to cook it:

1. Preheat the Omni toaster oven to 400 degrees F in Toast mode
2. Line a baking sheet with parchment paper
3. Place all Ingredients your food processor
4. Pulse until smooth
5. Scoop a tablespoon of mixture and place on baking sheet
6. Toast for 25 minutes
7. Serve and enjoy!

Nutritional value per serving:

Calories: 100 kcal, Protein: 7g, Fat: 5g, Carbs: 7g

Thai Sesame Edamame

The most authentic Edamame recipe from Thailand, try it out. You won't be disappointed!

Prep time and cooking time: 1 hour 20 minutes | Serves: 4

Ingredients To Use:

- 4 cups edamame pods
- 1 teaspoon sesame seeds, toasted
- 1 tablespoon rice vinegar
- 1 tablespoon dark sesame oil
- 1/2 teaspoon black pepper, ground
- 1/2 teaspoon salt
- 3 tablespoons water

Step-by-Step Directions to cook it:

1. Preheat your Omni Toaster Oven to 300 degrees F in bake mode
2. Line a baking sheet with aluminum foil
3. Set it aside
4. Take a bowl and add all Ingredients
5. Toss to coat the edamame pods with the seasoning
6. Arrange the seasoned edamame pods in the baking sheet
7. Bake for 1 hour and 10 minutes
8. Serve and enjoy!

Nutritional value per serving:

Calories: 150 kcal, Protein: 11g, Fat: 8g, Carbs: 10g

Curry Cauliflower Toasted Pistachio

While pistachio might not be everyone's cup of tea, if you mix it up with some curried cauliflower, you are gonna find it irresistible!
Prep time and cooking time: 30 minutes | Serves: 4

Ingredients To Use:

- 7 ounces cauliflower, thinly sliced
- 2 tablespoons extra virgin coconut oil
- A handful of pistachios, crushed
- 1 tablespoon mustard seed
- 1/2 red onion, thinly sliced
- 1 teaspoon curry powder
- Salt to taste

Step-by-Step Directions to cook it:

1. Preheat your Omni Toaster Oven to 350 degrees F in toast mode
2. Take a pan and combine everything to coat the cauliflower with seasoning
3. Place the cauliflower on a baking dish
4. Lined with aluminum foil
5. Toast in the Toaster Oven for 20 minutes
6. Serve and enjoy!

Nutritional value per serving:

Calories: 510 kcal, Protein: 15g, Fat: 43g, Carbs: 23g

Garbanzo Bean Meal

The best Garbanzo meal you are gonna find out there! And the best part? Since it's made using your Toaster Oven, it has minimal oil and maximum taste!

Prep time and cooking time: 40 minutes | Serves: 4

Ingredients To Use:

- 1 can garbanzo beans, chickpeas
- 1 tablespoon olive oil
- 1 teaspoon sunflower seeds
- 1 teaspoon garlic powder
- 1/2 teaspoon paprika

Step-by-Step Directions to cook it:

1. Pre-heat your Omni Toaster Oven to 375 degrees F in Bake Mode
2. Line a baking sheet with silicone baking mat
3. Drain and rinse garbanzo beans, pat garbanzo beans dry and pout into a large bowl
4. Toss with olive oil, sunflower seeds, garlic powder, paprika and mix well
5. Spread over a baking sheet
6. Bake for 20 minutes at 375 degrees F
7. Turn chickpeas, so they are roasted well
8. Place back in Toaster Oven and bake for 25 minutes at 375 degrees F
9. Let them cool and enjoy!

Nutritional value per serving:

Calories: 200 kcal, Protein: 25g, Fat: 25g, Carbs: 36g

Roasted Garlic Soup

If you are feeling a little blue, this garlic soup is what you need!
Prep time and cooking time: 70 minutes | Serves: 4

Ingredients To Use:

- 1 tablespoon olive oil
- 2 bulbs garlic, peeled
- 3 shallots, chopped
- 1 large head cauliflower, chopped
- 6 cups vegetable broth
- Sunflower seeds and pepper to taste

Step-by-Step Directions to cook it:

1. Pre-heat your Omni Toaster Oven to 400 degrees F in Bake Mode
2. Slice 1/4 inch top of the garlic bulb and place it in an aluminum foil
3. Grease with olive oil and roast in Toaster Oven for 35 minutes
4. Squeeze flesh out of the roasted garlic
5. Heat oil in a saucepan and add shallots, Sauté for 6 minutes
6. Add garlic and remaining Ingredients:
7. Cover the pan and lower down the heat to low
8. Let it cook for 15-20 minutes
9. Use an immersion blender to puree the mixture
10. Season soup with sunflower seeds and pepper
11. Serve and enjoy!

Nutritional value per serving:

Calories: 300 kcal, Protein: 25g, Fat: 25g, Carbs: 36g

Cayenne Sweet Potato And Cumin

Italian potato meal with some added cumin, awesome till the last crunch!

Prep time and cooking time: 30 minutes | Serves: 4

Ingredients To Use:

- 1 teaspoon butter
- 1 teaspoon rosemary
- Salt and pepper to taste
- 2 garlic cloves, minced
- 4 potatoes, washed

Step-by-Step Directions to cook it:

1. In a bowl, mix olive oil, salt, garlic powder, chili powder, and cumin. Add in potatoes and toss to coat.
2. Arrange them on the basket and fit in the baking tray.
3. Cook in your Toaster Oven for 20 minutes at 380 F on Air Fry function.
4. Toss every 5 minutes. Sprinkle with parsley and serve.

Nutritional value per serving:

Calories: 245 kcal, Protein: 3g, Fat: 10g, Carbs: 40g

Jalapeno Tomato Gratin

While most people go after potato gratin, why not go after something a bit more "Offbeat"? Just what you need!
Prep time and cooking time: 40 minutes | Serves: 4

Ingredients To Use:

- 1 can tomato sauce
- 1/2 cup milk
- 2 large eggs, beaten
- 2 tablespoons all-purpose flour
- 1 cup Monetary Jack cheese, shredded
- 1 cup cheddar cheese shredded
- 1 can jalapeno pepper

Step-by-Step Directions to cook it:

1. Preheat Omni Toaster Oven on Air Fry function to 380 F.
2. Arrange the jalapeño peppers on the greased Air Fryer baking pan and top with half of the cheese.
3. In a medium bowl, combine the eggs, milk, and flour and pour the mixture over the chilies—Cook in your Toaster Oven for 20 minutes.
4. Take out the chilies and pour the tomato sauce over them.
5. Return and cook for 15 more minutes. Sprinkle with the remaining cheese and serve.

Nutritional value per serving:

Calories: 221 kcal, Protein: 5g, Fat: 18g, Carbs: 12g

Cheesy Vegetable Frittata

A frittata that is both cheesy and healthy, packed with veggies?
Sign me up!
Prep time and cooking time: 40 minutes | Serves: 4

Ingredients To Use:

- 1/3 cup feta cheese, crumbled
- 1/3 cup cheddar cheese, crumbled
- Salt and pepper to taste
- 1/3 cup milk
- 4 eggs, cracked in a bowl
- 2 teaspoon olive oil
- 1/4 pound asparagus, trimmed and sliced
- 1 small red onion, sliced
- 1/4 cup chives, chopped
- 1/3 cup mushrooms, sliced
- 1 zucchini, sliced
- 1 cup baby spinach

Step-by-Step Directions to cook it:

1. Preheat Omni Toaster Oven on Bake function to 320 degrees F.
2. Line a baking dish with parchment paper. Mix the beaten eggs with milk, salt, and pepper. Heat olive oil in a skillet over medium heat add stir-fry asparagus, zucchini, onion, mushrooms, and baby spinach for 5 minutes.
3. Pour the veggies into the baking dish and top with the egg mixture. Sprinkle with feta and cheddar cheeses.
4. Cook for 15 minutes. Garnish with chives.

Nutritional value per serving:

Calories: 160 kcal, Protein: 10g, Fat: 11g, Carbs: 9g

Coconut Flavored Macaroons

These macaroons have the perfect balance of coconut and maple to give a very tasty, naturally sweet flavor.

Prep time and cooking time: 30 minutes | Serves: 4

Ingredients To Use:

- 1 and 1/4 cups coconut, shredded
- 1/4 cup walnut flour
- 1/4 cup maple syrup
- 3 tablespoons olive oil

Step-by-Step Directions to cook it:

1. Preheat your Omni Toaster Oven to 320 degrees F in Air Fry mode
2. Line a baking sheet with parchment
3. Take a food processor and add ingredients, pulse well
4. Scoop mixture into balls
5. Transfer to a baking sheet and transfer to Toaster Oven cooking basket
6. Bake for 10-15 minutes
7. Serve and enjoy!

Nutritional value per serving:

Calories: 90 kcal, Protein: 0.8g, Fat: 7g, Carbs: 6g

BBQ Zucchini Delight

Why do you always have to go with meat steak when you can go with some flavorful Zucchini ones, right?

Prep time and cooking time: 70 minutes | Serves: 4

Ingredients To Use:

- Olive oil as needed
- 3 zucchinis
- 1/2 teaspoon black pepper
- 1/2 teaspoon mustard
- 1/2 teaspoon cumin
- 1 teaspoon paprika
- 1 teaspoon garlic powder
- 1 tablespoon of sea salt
- 1-2 stevia
- 1 tablespoon chili powder

Step-by-Step Directions to cook it:

1. Preheat your Omni Toaster Oven to 300 degrees F in Bake Mode
2. Take a small bowl and add cayenne, black pepper, salt, garlic, mustard, paprika, chili powder, and stevia
3. Mix well
4. Slice zucchini into 1/8 inch slices and mist them with olive oil
5. Sprinkle spice blend over zucchini and bake for 40 minutes
6. Remove and flip, mist with more olive oil and leftover spice
7. Bake for 20 minutes more
8. Serve!

Nutritional value per serving:

Calories: 163 kcal, Protein: 8g, Fat: 14g, Carbs: 3g

Chapter 7: Air Fryer Recipes

Simple Boiled Eggs

The classic boiled egg, nothing fancy! Protein-packed delight.
Prep time and cooking time: 20 minutes | Serves: 6

Ingredients To Use:

- 6 large eggs

Step-by-Step Directions to cook it:

1. Preheat your Omni to 300 degrees F in Air Fry mode
2. Put the eggs in a single layer in your air fryer basket carefully.
3. Bake for at least 8 minutes for a slightly runny yolk.
4. Or 12 to 15 minutes for a firmer yolk.
5. Using tongs, remove the eggs from the air fryer carefully.
6. Then take a bowl of very cold water and immediately place them in it.
7. Let the eggs stand in the cold water for 5 minutes, then gently crack the shell underwater.
8. After that, let the eggs stand for another minute or two, then peel and eat.
9. Enjoy!

Nutritional value per serving:

Calories: 63 kcal, Protein: 6g, Fat: 4g, Carbs: 1g

Bread And Berry Platter

Wake up and start your day with a meal straight from the dining table of a French family. This French toast is a dreamy delight for those who are looking for something a little bit sweet with bites of crunch and berry goodness.

Prep time and cooking time: 15 minutes | Serves: 2

Ingredients To Use:

- 2 large whole eggs
- 1 teaspoon vanilla extract
- 2 thick slices sourdough
- A squeeze of honey
- 2 teaspoons low-fat Greek yogurt

Step-by-Step Directions to cook it:

1. Pre-heat your Omin in Air Fryer mode to a temperature of 356 degrees Fahrenheit
2. Take a bowl and beat your eggs well
3. Add vanilla to the egg and mix well
4. Take the bread and carefully butter both sides of the bread
5. Soak the bread in your egg mix and soak it until it has properly absorbed the mix
6. Take out the Air Fryer cooking basket and place the bread on top
7. Allow them to cook for about 6 minutes, making sure to give the bread a turn halfway through
8. Once done, serve the bread with some yogurt, berries, and honey

Nutritional value per serving:

Calories: 90 kcal, Protein: 4g, Fat: 2g, Carbs: 18g

Classic French Toast

The original French Toast, you are gonna keep coming back for more!

Prep time and cooking time: 15 minutes | Serves: 4

Ingredients To Use:

- 4 bread slices
- 2 tablespoons butter
- 2 beaten eggs
- Salt and pepper as needed
- Cinnamon as needed
- Nutmeg as needed
- Ground clove spices, as needed
- Icing sugar for garnish
- Maple syrup for garnish

Step-by-Step Directions to cook it:

1. Preheat your Omin to 360-degree F in Air Fryer mode
2. Take a bowl and add eggs, beat well
3. Season egg mix with cinnamon and nutmeg
4. Add ground cloves and mix
5. Take bread slices and butter both sides
6. Dredge them in the mixture
7. Arrange in your Air Fryer cooking basket and cook for 6 minutes
8. Serve and enjoy!

Nutritional value per serving:

Calories: 124 kcal, Protein: 8g, Fat: 1g, Carbs: 25g

Awesome Potato Pancakes

Who doesn't love a healthy dose of pancakes to start off the day with? With the following recipe, batch up a nice proportion of potato pancakes during the day!
Prep time and cooking time: 30-35 minutes | Serves: 2

Ingredients To Use:

- 4 medium potatoes, peeled and cleaned
- 1 medium onion, chopped
- 1 beaten egg
- 1/4 cup milk
- 1/2 teaspoon garlic powder
- 2 tablespoons unsalted butter
- 1/4 teaspoon salt
- 3 tablespoons all-purpose flour
- Pepper as needed

Step-by-Step Directions to cook it:

1. Peel your potatoes and shred them up
2. Soak the shredded potatoes under cold water to remove starch
3. Drain the potatoes
4. Take a bowl and add eggs, milk, butter, garlic powder, salt, and pepper
5. Add in flour
6. Mix well
7. Add the shredded potatoes
8. Preheat your Omin in Air Fryer mode to a temperature of 390 degrees Fahrenheit
9. Add 1/4 cup of the potato pancake batter to your cooking basket and cook for 12 minutes until the golden brown texture is seen
10. Enjoy!

Nutritional value per serving:

Calories: 243 kcal, Protein: 6g, Fat: 11g, Carbs: 33g

Cool Bacon Muffin

Who doesn't love muffins? Were you afraid that going all healthy might need to sacrifice cupcakes? Well, don't be afraid as here with this recipe, you will be able to cook up delicious cupcakes in no time! Suitable for your feisty meal.

Prep time and cooking time: 20 minutes | Serves: 2

Ingredients To Use:

- 1 whole egg
- 2 streaky bacon
- 1 English muffin
- Salt and pepper to taste

Step-by-Step Directions to cook it:

1. Preheat your Air Fryer to 200 degrees F
2. Take an ovenproof bowl and crack in the egg
3. Take Air Fryer cooking basket and add bacon, egg, and muffin into Fryer
4. Cook for 7 minutes
5. Assemble muffin done by packing bacon and egg on top of English muffin
6. Serve and enjoy!

Nutritional value per serving:

Calories: 500 kcal, Protein: 24g, Fat: 48g, Carbs: 38g

Hearty Morning Mac

The classic Mac And Cheese re-defined for the Omni Toaster Oven!
Prep time and cooking time: 20 minutes | Serves: 2

Ingredients To Use:

- 1 cup elbow macaroni
- 1/2 cup broccoli
- 1/2 cup warmed milk
- 1 and 1/2 cheddar cheese, grated
- Salt and pepper to taste
- 1 tablespoon parmesan cheese, grated

Step-by-Step Directions to cook it:

1. Pre-heat your Omni in Air Fry mode to 400 degrees F
2. Take a pot and add water, allow it to boil
3. Add macaroni and veggies and broil for about 10 minutes until the mixture is Al Dente
4. Drain the pasta and vegetables
5. Toss the pasta and veggies with cheese
6. Season with some pepper and salt and transfer the mixture to your Fryer
7. Sprinkle some more parmesan on top and cook for about 15 minutes.
8. Allow it to cool for about 10 minutes once done
9. Enjoy!

Nutritional value per serving:

Calories: 153 kcal, Protein: 6g, Fat: 11g, Carbs: 14g

Delicious Cheese Omelette

Craving for some cheesy omelet? This just what you need!
Prep time and cooking time: 20 minutes | Serves: 2

Ingredients To Use:

- 2 whole eggs
- Salt and pepper to taste
- 1 tablespoon cheddar cheese
- 1 onion, sliced
- 1 teaspoon coconut aminos

Step-by-Step Directions to cook it:

1. Preheat your Omni in Air Fryer mode up to 340 degrees F
2. Clean and chop onion
3. Take a plate and cover with 2 teaspoon aminos
4. Transfer into the Air Fryer and cook for 8 minutes
5. Beat eggs and add pepper with salt
6. Pour the egg mixture on onions and cook the mix in your Air Fryer for 3 minutes more
7. Add cheddar cheese and bake for 2 minutes more
8. Serve with fresh basil leaves
9. Enjoy!

Nutritional value per serving:

Calories: 400 kcal, Protein: 27g, Fat: 23g, Carbs: 1g

Authentic Grilled Cheese Sandwich

Boot up your systems after a long day with a classic grilled sandwich!

Prep time and cooking time: 15 minutes | Serves: 2

Ingredients To Use:

- 2 bread slices
- 2 cheese slices
- 2 teaspoons butter

Step-by-Step Directions to cook it:

1. Pre-heat your Omni in Air Fry mode to a temperature of 350-degree Fahrenheit
2. But the bread slices carefully
3. Place a cheese slice on the unbuttered side of bread
4. Keep repeating until your bread are prepared
5. Place the prepared bread in your Air Fryer cooking basket
6. Cook for 10 minutes (making sure to flip once after 5 minutes)
7. Enjoy!

Nutritional value per serving:

Calories: 400 kcal, Protein: 14g, Fat: 23g, Carbs: 30g

Herby Mushroom Roast

An Eccentric mushroom dish for all the mushroom lovers out there!
Prep time and cooking time: 40 minutes | Serves: 4

Ingredients To Use:

- 1 cup walnuts, soaked
- 1 garlic clove, chopped
- 1 tablespoon lemon juice
- 1/2 teaspoon salt
- 1/4 teaspoon pepper
- 1/4 cup dill, chopped
- 1/4 cup fresh parsley, chopped
- 1/4 teaspoon cayenne pepper
- 10 mushrooms, stems removed
- 5 cherry tomatoes, halved

Step-by-Step Directions to cook it:

1. Preheat your Omni in Air Fryer mode to 320 degrees F
2. Take a baking dish and line with parchment paper
3. Add nuts, clove, juice, salt to a food processor and blend until smooth
4. Add cayenne, dill, parsley and blend more
5. Stuff mushroom with the mix
6. Transfer them to your baking dish
7. Transfer baking dish to Air fryer cooking basket
8. Cook for 12-15 minutes until soft
9. Serve and enjoy!

Nutritional value per serving:

Calories: 219 kcal, Protein: 6g, Fat: 18g, Carbs: 6g

Hearty Feta Quiche

The original cheesy quiche for that late-night craving in the middle of the night!
Prep time and cooking time: 50 minutes | Serves: 4

Ingredients To Use:

- 12 ounces thawed puff pastry
- 4 large eggs
- 1/4 cup milk
- 1 medium zucchini, sliced
- 4 ounces feta, drained and crumbled
- 1 medium zucchini, sliced
- 2 tablespoons fresh dill, chopped
- Olive oil spray as needed
- Salt and pepper as needed

Step-by-Step Directions to cook it:

1. Pre-heat your Omni in Air Fry mode to a temperature of 360-degree Fahrenheit
2. Take a bowl and beat in eggs
3. Season the egg with salt and pepper
4. Add zucchini, feta cheese, and dill
5. Give it a stir
6. Take 8 muffin tins and grease them well
7. Roll out your pastry and cover the bottom and sides of your muffin tin with the pastry
8. Pour the egg mix amongst the muffins and cook them in batches
9. Each batch should go for 15-20 minutes until the crust is golden
10. Transfer them to your serving plate and enjoy!

Nutritional value per serving:

Calories: 140 kcal, Protein: 4g, Fat: 8g, Carbs: 11g

Chapter 8: Baking And Toasting Recipes

Cool Quinoa Squash

It's a really sad fact that many people still hate quinoa! Even though it is possibly one of the healthiest grain out there. Well, this herbed quinoa might just change their perspective!

Prep time and cooking time: 35 minutes | Serves: 4

Ingredients To Use:

- 1 teaspoon ginger, minced
- 2 teaspoons thyme
- 1 and 1/2 cups quinoa
- 1/4 cup walnuts, chopped
- 2 onions, sliced
- 1 red bell pepper
- 2 tablespoons olive oil
- 1 big spaghetti squash
- Salt and pepper to taste

Step-by-Step Directions to cook it:

1. Preheat your Toaster Oven to 380 degrees F in Air Fry mode
2. Clean squash, slice in half
3. Transfer to Toaster Oven cooking basket and cook for 30-40 minutes until tender
4. Take a skillet and heat a tablespoon oil, add bell pepper, quinoa, onion, walnuts and cook until warm
5. Season well with salt and pepper
6. Divide mixture between squash and bake for 2-5 minutes more
7. Serve and enjoy!

Nutritional value per serving:

Calories: 429 kcal, Protein: 13g, Fat: 22g, Carbs: 49g

Apple Pie Crackers

Crispy, crunchy baked crackers, you will love them even if you are not a parrot!

Prep time and cooking time: 30 minutes | Serves: 100 crackers

Ingredients To Use:

- 2 tablespoons + 2 teaspoons avocado oil
- 1 medium Granny Smith apple, roughly chopped
- 1/4 cup Erythritol
- 1/4 cup sunflower seeds, ground
- 1 and 3/4 cups roughly ground flax seeds
- 1/8 teaspoon ground cloves
- 1/8 teaspoon ground cardamom
- 3 tablespoons nutmeg
- 1/4 teaspoon ground ginger

Step-by-Step Directions to cook it:

1. Pre-heat your Omni Toaster Oven to 225 degrees F in Bake Mode
2. Line two baking sheets with parchment paper and keep them on the side
3. Add oil, apple, Erythritol to a bowl and mix
4. Transfer to a food processor and add remaining ingredients, process until combined
5. Transfer batter to baking sheets spread evenly and cut into crackers
6. Bake for 1 hour, flip and bake for another hour
7. Let them cool and serve
8. Enjoy!

Nutritional value per serving:

Calories: 1 kcal, Protein: 0.4g, Fat: 2g, Carbs: 0.9g

Delicious Herby Buns

The classic healthy herbed buns go great as a base for mini burgers!
Prep time and cooking time: 25 minutes | Serves: 4

Ingredients To Use:

- 4 whole eggs
- 1/4 cup arrowroot flour
- 1/3 cup coconut flour
- 1 teaspoon baking powder
- 1/4 teaspoon onion powder
- 1/4 teaspoon garlic powder
- 1/4 teaspoon dried parsley
- 1/4 teaspoon oregano
- 1/4 teaspoon dried basil
- 1/4 teaspoon salt
- 1/4 cup butter, melted

Step-by-Step Directions to cook it:

1. Pre-heat your Omni Toaster Oven to 350 degrees F in Bake Mode
2. Line a baking sheet with parchment paper and keep it on the side
3. Take a bowl and whisk in eggs, arrowroot, coconut flour, and baking powder
4. Mix well
5. Add seasoning and butter
6. Stir well, give the batter a nice mix
7. Use 1/3 cup an as a measure to make 6 mounds, arranging them on your prepped baking sheet
8. Bake in your Toaster Oven for 15 minutes
9. Remove from Toaster Oven and let it cool
10. Serve and enjoy!

Nutritional value per serving:

Calories: 10 kcal, Protein: 4g, Fat: 10g, Carbs: 10g

Lovely Cauliflower Bagels

Want bagel a want them in healthy form? Just go with these!
Prep time and cooking time: 40 minutes | Serves: 12

Ingredients To Use:

- 1 large cauliflower, divided into florets and roughly chopped
- 1/4 cup nutritional yeast
- 1/4 cup almond flour
- 1/2 teaspoon garlic powder
- 1 and 1/2 teaspoon fine sea salt
- 2 whole eggs
- 1 tablespoon sesame seeds

Step-by-Step Directions to cook it:

1. Pre-heat your Omni Toaster Oven to 400 degrees F in Bake Mode
2. Line a baking sheet with parchment paper, keep it on the side
3. Blend cauliflower in a food processor and transfer to a bowl
4. Add nutritional yeast, almond flour, garlic powder and salt to a bowl, mix
5. Take another bowl and whisk in eggs, add to cauliflower mix
6. Give the dough a stir
7. Incorporate the mix into the egg mix
8. Make balls from the dough, making a hole using your thumb into each ball
9. Arrange them on your prepped sheet, flattening them into bagel shapes
10. Sprinkle sesame seeds and bake for 1/2 an hour
11. Remove Toaster Oven and let them cool, enjoy!

Nutritional value per serving:

Calories: 2 kcal, Protein: 2g, Fat: 6g, Carbs: 1.5g

Simple Baked Bread Loaf

The simplest bread loaf recipe to kick start your baking life!
Prep time and cooking time: 40 minutes | Serves: 20 slices

Ingredients To Use:

- 6 eggs, whites separated
- 1/4 teaspoon cream of tartar
- 4 tablespoons butter, melted
- 3 teaspoons baking powder
- 1 and 1/2 cup of almond flour
- Pinch of salt

Step-by-Step Directions to cook it:

1. Pre-heat your Omni Toaster Oven to 375 degrees F in Bake Mode
2. Take an 8x4 inch loaf pan and grease it, keep it on the side
3. Take a bowl and beat egg whites, cream of tartar until a soft peak starts to form
4. Keep the mix on the side
5. Take a food processor and mix butter, egg yolks, baking powder, almond flour, and salt
6. Add 1/3 of egg whites to food processor and pulse until combined
7. Add rest of the egg whites and mix until combined
8. Transfer dough to the prepared loaf pan and bake for 30 minutes
9. Let it cool and slice, enjoy!

Nutritional value per serving:

Calories: 170 kcal, Protein: 5g, Fat: 22g, Carbs: 16g

Fancy Cinnamon Bread Meal

Modify the flavor of the basic bread meal with the addition of some cinnamon, wicked!

Prep time and cooking time: 40 minutes | Serves: 10 slices

Ingredients To Use:

- 3 pastured eggs
- 1 teaspoon vinegar
- 3 tablespoons salted butter
- 2 tablespoons water
- 1/2 cup coconut flour
- 1/2 teaspoon baking soda
- 1 teaspoon cinnamon
- 1/2 teaspoon baking powder
- 1/3 cup pure sour cream
- 1/8 teaspoon stevia

Step-by-Step Directions to cook it:

1. Pre-heat your Omni Toaster Oven to 350 degrees F in Bake Mode
2. Take a loaf pan and oil it, line the bottom with parchment paper
3. Mix dry ingredients in a bowl and whisk well
4. Add remaining ingredients to the dry mix and mix well, taste for sweetness
5. Adjust seasoning
6. Let the mix stand for 3 minutes
7. Spread batter onto loaf pan and bake for 25-30 minutes
8. Cool loaf, and enjoy it!

Nutritional value per serving:

Calories: 468 kcal, Protein: 11g, Fat: 45g, Carbs: 17 g

Homely Thanksgiving Bread

The perfect baked bread for a thanksgiving dinner.
Prep time and cooking time: 40 minutes | Serves: 4

Ingredients To Use:

- 1/4 teaspoon of sea salt
- 1/2 cup chicken broth
- 1/2 cup walnuts
- 1/2 cup coconut flour
- 1 onion, chopped
- 1 tablespoon fresh rosemary, chopped
- 1 teaspoon baking soda
- 1 tablespoon grass-fed organic ghee
- 10 sage leaves, finely chopped
- 1 and 1/2 cups almond flour
- 2 stalks celery, chopped
- Pinch of nutmeg, freshly grated

Step-by-Step Directions to cook it:

1. Pre-heat your Omni Toaster Oven to 350 degrees F in Bake Mode
2. Add ghee to the pan and melt over medium heat
3. Add celery, onion to the pan and Saute for 5 minutes
4. Add walnuts, Saute for few minutes
5. Add nutmeg, rosemary sage, salt, baking soda, coconut flour, almond flour in a large bowl and mix
6. Add Sautéed onion in a large bowl alongside dried ingredients, alongside broth and eggs
7. Mix until you have a nice batter
8. Fold in bacon
9. Spread thick batter onto loaf pan and bake for 35 minutes
10. Once a toothpick comes out, clean, serve, and enjoy!

Nutritional value per serving:

Calories: 339 kcal, Protein: 13g, Fat: 26g, Carbs: 16g

Baked Bacon Fat Bombs

Bacon fat Bombs packed with all the protein goodness that you need for your next workout!

Prep time and cooking time: 55 minutes | Serves: 4

Ingredients To Use:

- 2 whole large eggs, boiled, peeled and cut into quarters
- 1/4 cup butter
- 2 tablespoons mayonnaise
- 4 large slices of bacon
- Salt and pepper to taste

Step-by-Step Directions to cook it:

1. Pre-heat your Omni Toasted Oven to 375 degrees F in Bake Mode
2. Take a baking tray and lay the bacon strips, bake for 15 minutes and reserve the grease for later use
3. Cut butter into pieces and add them to a bowl
4. Add quartered eggs and mash the whole mixture until mixed
5. Add remaining ingredients to the butter egg mix (except bacon) and mix
6. Pour bacon grease and mix again
7. Let the mixture chill for 30 minutes
8. Top with crumbled bacon and make 6 balls using the mixture
9. Enjoy!

Nutritional value per serving:

Calories: 209 kcal, Protein: 4g, Fat: 21g, Carbs: 1g

Awesome Almond Munchies

Crispy almond munchies, your new best friend!
Prep time and cooking time: 75 minutes | Serves: 20 crackers

Ingredients To Use:

- 1/2 cup ground flax seeds
- 1/2 cup almond flour
- 1 tablespoon coconut flour
- 2 tablespoons shelled hemp seeds
- 1/4 teaspoon sea salt, plus more to sprinkle on top
- 1 egg white
- 2 tablespoons unsalted butter, melted

Step-by-Step Directions to cook it:

1. Preheat your Omni Toaster Oven to 300 degrees F in Bake Mode
2. Take a baking sheet and line it with parchment paper, keep the prepared sheet on the side
3. Add flax, coconut flour, almond, salt, hemp seed to a bowl and mix well
4. Add egg and melted butter, mix well
5. Transfer dough to a sheet of parchment paper and cover with another sheet of paper
6. Roll out dough
7. Cut into crackers and bake for 60 minutes
8. Cool and serve!

Nutritional value per serving:

Calories: 47 kcal, Protein: 2g, Fat: 6g, Carbs: 1.2g

Toasted Chipotle Kale Chips

Want a healthier chip? These Kale chips are the ones that you need!
Prep time and cooking time: 25 minutes | Serves: 4

Ingredients To Use:

- 2 large bunch kale, chopped into 4 pieces and stemmed
- 1 tablespoon olive oil
- 1/8 teaspoon salt
- 1 teaspoon chipotle powder
- 1/4 cup cashew cheese

Step-by-Step Directions to cook it:

1. Wash kale thoroughly and dry, cut into 4-inch pieces
2. Pre-heat your Omni Toaster Oven to 250 degrees F in toast mode
3. Take a baking sheet and line with parchment paper
4. Take a bowl and add kale, coat the kale with olive oil, chipotle, and cheese
5. Transfer the mix to a baking sheet
6. Toast for 15 minutes and check the crispiness
7. If you need more crispiness, bake for 9 minutes more
8. Serve and enjoy!

Nutritional value per serving:

Calories: 40 kcal, Protein: 1g, Fat: 3g, Carbs: 2g

Elegant Sweet Potato Meal

Sweet potatoes with some red wine vinegar and Italian seasoning added? What could possibly go wrong?

Prep time and cooking time: 30 minutes | Serves: 4

Ingredients To Use:

- 1 large sweet potato, peeled and sliced
- pound Brussels sprouts, trimmed
- 1 tablespoon red wine vinegar
- 2 cloves garlic, minced
- 1/3 cup olive oil
- 1 teaspoon cumin
- 1/4 teaspoon salt
- 1/4 teaspoon black pepper

Step-by-Step Directions to cook it:

1. Preheat your Omni Toaster Oven to 400 degrees F in toast mode
2. Take a bowl and place all ingredients
3. Toss to coat well
4. Take a baking pan and transfer it
5. Lined with aluminum foil
6. Toast for 20 minutes
7. Serve and enjoy!

Nutritional value per serving:

Calories: 168 kcal, Protein: 3g, Fat: 12g, Carbs: 14g

Delicious Chocolate Toasted Bacon

What's better than traditional bacon? Having chocolate-coated toasty bacon, of course!

Prep time and cooking time: 35 minutes | Serves: 4

Ingredients To Use:

- 12 bacon slices
- 4 and 1/2 tablespoons unsweetened dark chocolate
- 2 and 1/4 tablespoons coconut oil
- 1 and 1/2 teaspoons liquid stevia

Step-by-Step Directions to cook it:

1. Pre-heat you Omni Toaster Oven to 425 degrees F in Toast Mode
2. Skewer bacon into iron skewers
3. Arrange skewers on a baking sheet and toast for 15 minutes until they show a crispy texture
4. Transfer to a cooling rack
5. Take a saucepan and place it over low heat, add coconut oil and let it melt
6. Stir in coconut chocolate and heat until it melts
7. Add stevia and gently stir
8. Place crispy bacon on parchment paper and drizzle chocolate mix
9. Let the chocolate harden
10. Serve!

Nutritional value per serving:

Calories: 256 kcal, Protein: 7g, Fat: 26g, Carbs: 0.5g

Toasted Balsamic Baby Carrots

The awesome balsamic baby carrots are here at your service! Just go ahead, make a batch for your kids and family!
Prep time and cooking time: 25 minutes | Serves: 4

Ingredients To Use:

- 1 and 1/2 pounds baby carrots, peeled
- 2 tablespoons balsamic vinegar
- 2 tablespoons olive oil
- A pinch parsley
- A pinch salt
- A pinch pepper

Step-by-Step Directions to cook it:

1. Preheat your Omni Toaster Oven to 400 degrees F in Toast mode
2. Take a bowl and place all ingredients
3. Toss to coat well
4. Take a baking pan and transfer it
5. Lined with aluminum foil
6. Toast for 20 minutes
7. Serve and enjoy!

Nutritional value per serving:

Calories: 128 kcal, Protein: 1g, Fat: 7g, Carbs: 15

Mediterranean Tilapia

The original Mediterranean Tilapia dish recipe! What are you waiting for? Jump right in!

Prep time and cooking time: 30 minutes | Serves: 4

Ingredients To Use:

- 3 tablespoons sun-dried tomatoes, packed in oil, drained and chopped
- 1 tablespoon capers, drained
- 2 tilapia fillets
- 1 tablespoon oil from sun-dried tomatoes
- 2 tablespoons kalamata olives, chopped and pitted

Step-by-Step Directions to cook it:

1. Pre-heat your Toaster Oven to 372 degrees Fahrenheit in Toast mode
2. Take a small-sized bowl and add sun-dried tomatoes, olives, capers and stir well
3. Keep the mixture on the side
4. Take a baking sheet and transfer the tilapia fillets and arrange them side by side
5. Drizzle olive oil all over them
6. Toast in your Toaster Oven for 10-15 minutes
7. After 10 minutes, check the fish for a "Flaky" texture
8. Once cooked properly, top the fish with tomato mixture and serve!

Nutritional value per serving:

Calories: 180 kcal, Protein: 92g, Fat: 8g, Carbs: 18g

Crispy Fancy Shrimp

Crispy, tasty shrimp dish. The perfect toasted dish for your expensive shrimps!

Prep time and cooking time: 20 minutes | Serves: 4

Ingredients To Use:

- 1/2 ounces large shrimp, peeled and deveined
- Cooking spray as needed
- 1 teaspoon low sodium coconut aminos
- 1 teaspoon parsley
- 1/2 teaspoon olive oil
- 1/2 tablespoon honey
- 1 tablespoon lemon juice

Step-by-Step Directions to cook it:

1. Pre-heat your Omni Toaster Oven to 450 degrees F in Toast Mode
2. Take a baking dish and grease it well
3. Mix in all the ingredients and toss
4. Transfer to Toaster Oven and bake for 8 minutes until shrimp turn pink
5. Serve and enjoy!

Nutritional value per serving:

Calories: 284 kcal, Protein: 32g, Fat: 18g, Carbs: 1g

Chapter 9: Dehydrating Recipes

Awesome Dehydrated Beet Chips

Simple and easy dehydrated beet chips, just go ahead and give it a try!

Prep time and cooking time: 8 hours | Serves: 4

Ingredients To Use:

- 1/2 beet, cut into 1/8 inch slices

Step-by-Step Directions to cook it:

1. Arrange beet slices in a single layer in the cooking basket
2. Place the basket in your Omni Toaster Oven
3. Press the Dehydrate button and let it dehydrate for 8 hours at 135 degrees F
4. Once the dehydrating is done, remove the basket from pot and transfer slices to your Air Tight container, serve and enjoy!

Nutritional value per serving:

Calories: 35 kcal, Protein: 1g, Fat: 0g, Carbs: 8g

Squash Chips

Bored of all the fat packed chips? Squash chips are what you need!
Prep time and cooking time: 12 hours | Serves: 4

Ingredients To Use:

- 2 cups yellow squash, sliced 1/8 inch thick
- 2 tablespoons apple cider vinegar
- 2 teaspoons olive oil
- Salt as needed

Step-by-Step Directions to cook it:

1. Take a mixing bowl and add squash slices, vinegar, oil and salt
2. Arrange squash slices on cooking single pan layer
3. Transfer to your Omni Toaster Oven
4. Cook on Dehydrate Mode in 110 F for 12 hours
5. Serve and enjoy!

Nutritional value per serving:

Calories: 15 kcal, Protein: 0.3g, Fat: 1.2g, Carbs: 1g

Kiwi Chips

You thought Kiwiw's were delicious on their own? Just wait till you try out some chips!
Prep time and cooking time: 10 hours | Serves: 4

Ingredients To Use:

- 6 kiwis, washed, patted dry

Step-by-Step Directions to cook it:

1. Arrange 1/4 inch thick slices on your cooking pan
2. Transfer to your Omni Toaster Oven
3. Cook on Dehydrate Mode in 135 F for 10 hours
4. Serve and enjoy!

Nutritional value per serving:

Calories: 70 kcal, Protein: 1.3g, Fat: 0.6g, Carbs: 16.7g

Smoked Eggplant Bacon

Who would've ever thought that smoked and dehydrated eggplant would taste so great, right? One munc, and you won't be able to stop!

Prep time and cooking time: 4 hours | Serves: 4

Ingredients To Use:

- 1 and 1/2 teaspoon smoked paprika
- 1/4 teaspoon garlic powder
- 1/4 teaspoon onion powder
- 1 medium eggplant

Step-by-Step Directions to cook it:

1. Cut eggplant into 1/4 inch thick slices
2. Toss eggplant and slices with onion powder, garlic powder, paprika in a bowl
3. Arrange eggplant slices on cooking pan in a single layer
4. Transfer Omni Toaster Oven
5. Cook on Dehydrate for 4 hours in 145 degrees F
6. Serve and enjoy!

Nutritional value per serving:

Calories: 32 kcal, Protein: 1.3g, Fat: 0.3g, Carbs: 8g

Toasty Pineapple Chunks

While Pizza's on pineapple are universally hated, dehydrated ones are absolute delights to eat!
Prep time and cooking time: 12 hours | Serves: 4

- 1 ripe pineapple, peel and cut in half

1. Cut pineapple into 1/4 inch thick chunks
2. Arrange pineapple chunks on cooking pan
3. Transfer to Omni Toaster Oven
4. Cook for 12 hours on Dehydrate mode at 135 degrees F
5. Serve and enjoy once done!

Calories: 21 kcal, Protein: 0.2g, Fat: 0.2g, Carbs: 5g

Asian Turkey Jerky

Who said chips are the only way to go when it comes to the dehydrator? Jerked turkeys will make your mouth water!
Prep time and cooking time: 5 hours | Serves: 4

Ingredients To Use:

- 1 lb. turkey meat, cut into thin slices
- 1-1/2 tsp. brown sugar
- 1/3 cup Worcestershire sauce
- 1/4 tsp. Tabasco sauce
- 1-1/2 tbsp. soy sauce
- 1 tbsp. liquid smoke
- 1-1/2 tsp. garlic powder
- 1/2 tbsp. onion powder
- 1 tsp. salt

Step-by-Step Directions to cook it:

1. Add listed ingredients except for turkey to a zip bag
2. Mix well, add turkey slices in the bag and shake
3. Let it sit overnight
4. Arrange marinade turkey slices on cooking basket
5. Transfer to Omni Toaster Oven and cook on Dehydrate in 160 degrees F for 5 hours
6. Serve and enjoy!

Nutritional value per serving:

Calories: 227 kcal, Protein: 33g, Fat: 6g, Carbs: 7g

Simple Beef Jerky

If you are bored of turkey jerky, just try out some beef ones!
Prep time and cooking time: 40 minutes | Serves: 4

Ingredients To Use:

- 1 tablespoon red pepper flakes
- 3/4 teaspoon liquid smoke
- 1/8 teaspoon cayenne pepper
- 1/2 cup of soy sauce
- 1/2 cup Worcestershire sauce
- 1 and 1/2 tablespoon ranch seasoning
- 1 pound flank steak, cut into thin slices

Step-by-Step Directions to cook it:

1. Add listed ingredients except for meat to a zip bag
2. Mix well, add meat slices in the bag and shake
3. Let it sit overnight
4. Arrange marinade meat slices on cooking basket
5. Transfer to Omni Toaster Oven and cook on Dehydrate in 145 degrees F for 8 hours
6. Serve and enjoy!

Nutritional value per serving:

Calories: 186 kcal, Protein: 22g, Fat: 6g, Carbs: 6g

Juicy Chicken Jerky

A creative way to dehydrate your chicken, store them up, and eat as a snack.

Prep time and cooking time 7 hours | Serves: 4

Ingredients To Use:

- 1/4 teaspoon pepper
- 1/4 teaspoon ground ginger
- 1/2 cup of soy sauce
- 1 teaspoon lemon juice
- 1/2 teaspoon garlic powder
- 1 pound chicken tenders, boneless and skinless, cut into ¼ inch slices

Step-by-Step Directions to cook it:

1. Add listed ingredients except for meat to a zip bag
2. Mix well, add meat slices in the bag and shake
3. Let it sit overnight
4. Arrange marinade meat slices on cooking basket
5. Transfer to Omni Toaster Oven and cook on Dehydrate in 145 degrees F for 7 hours
6. Serve and enjoy!

Nutritional value per serving:

Calories: 225 kcal, Protein: 34g, Fat: 9g, Carbs: 3g

Pork Jerky

Why should you always go for heavy pork recipes?
Prep time and cooking time: 5 hours | Serves: 4

- 1 teaspoon salt
- 1/2 teaspoon garlic powder
- 1/2 teaspoon oregano
- 1 teaspoon paprika
- 1/4 teaspoon pepper
- 1 teaspoon chili powder
- 1 pound pork lean meat, sliced

Step-by-Step Directions to cook it:

1. Add listed ingredients except for meat to a zip bag
2. Mix well, add meat slices in the bag and shake
3. Let it sit overnight
4. Arrange marinade meat slices on cooking basket
5. Transfer to Omni Toaster Oven and cook on Dehydrate in 160 degrees F for 5 hours
6. Serve and enjoy!

Nutritional value per serving:

Calories: 168 kcal, Protein: 29g, Fat: 4g, Carbs: 2g

Lamb Jerky

Since all the other meats are getting the limelight, why should lamb jerky stay out, right?

Prep time and cooking time: 40 minutes | Serves: 4

Ingredients To Use:

- 1 teaspoon garlic powder
- 1 tablespoon oregano
- 1/4 teaspoon pepper
- 1/3 cup soy sauce
- 2 tablespoons Worcestershire sauce
- 1 teaspoon onion powder
- 2 pounds boneless lamb, trimmed and cut into thin slices

Step-by-Step Directions to cook it:

1. Add listed ingredients except for meat to a zip bag
2. Mix well, add meat slices in the bag and shake
3. Let it sit overnight
4. Arrange marinade meat slices on cooking basket
5. Transfer to Omni Toaster Oven and cook on Dehydrate in 145 degrees F for 6 hours
6. Serve and enjoy!

Nutritional value per serving:

Calories: 300 kcal, Protein: 43g, Fat: 11g, Carbs: 3g

Cool Dry Bell Peppers

I've added a lot of jerkies! Now it's time for some dehydrated veggies, these bell peppers are the way to go!
Prep time and cooking time: 24 hours | Serves: 4

Ingredients To Use:

- 4 bell peppers, cut in half and seed removed

Step-by-Step Directions to cook it:

1. Cut bell pepper into strips, cut each strip into 1/2 inch pieces
2. Arrange bell pepper on cooking pan
3. Transfer to Omni Toaster Oven
4. Cook on Dehydrate mode for 24 hours at 135 degrees F
5. Serve and enjoy!

Nutritional value per serving:

Calories: 38 kcal, Protein: 1g, Fat: 0.3g, Carbs: 9g

Cinnamon Flavored Dehydrated Potatoes

The easiest and most wholesome dehydrated potato recipe you will find for your Omni appliance!
Prep time and cooking time: 12 hours | Serves: 4

Ingredients To Use:

- Salt as needed
- 1/8 teaspoon ground cinnamon
- 1 teaspoon coconut oil, melted
- 2 sweet potatoes, peeled and sliced thinly

Step-by-Step Directions to cook it:

1. Add sweet potato slices to the mixing bowl, add cinnamon, coconut oil, salt, and toss
2. Arrange sweet potato slices on cooking pan in a single layer
3. Place cooking pan in your Omni toaster Oven
4. Cook on Dehydrate mode at 125 degrees F for 12 hours

Nutritional value per serving:

Calories: 197 kcal, Protein: 2g, Fat: 2g, Carbs: 41g

Balsamic Zucchini Chips

The balsamic here really adds a lot of flavor to the dehydrated zucchini chips here!

Prep time and cooking time: 12 hours | Serves: 4

Ingredients To Use:

- 2 teaspoon salt
- 2 tablespoons balsamic vinegar
- 2 tablespoons olive oil
- 4 cups zucchini, cut into slices

Step-by-Step Directions to cook it:

1. Add olive oil, balsamic vinegar, salt to a large bowl
2. Stir well
3. Add sliced zucchini to the bowl and toss
4. Arrange slices on cooking pan, transfer to Omni toaster oven
5. Cook on Dehydrate mode for 12 hours at 135 degrees F
6. Serve and enjoy!

Nutritional value per serving:

Calories: 40 kcal, Protein: 0.7g, Fat: 3g, Carbs: 2g

Lovely Dehydrated Strawberries

Strawberries are really a symbol of sensuality and romanticism, dehydrating really takes things to the next level!
Prep time and cooking time: 12 hours | Serves: 4

Ingredients To Use:

- 2 cups strawberries, cut into 1/4 inch thick slices

Step-by-Step Directions to cook it:

1. Arrange strawberry slices on cooking pan in a single layer
2. Transfer to Omni Toaster Oven, dehydrate for 12 hours on 135 degrees F
3. Serve and enjoy!

Nutritional value per serving:

Calories: 20 kcal, Protein: 0.5g, Fat: 0.2g, Carbs: 5g

Fully Dehydrated Avocado Slices

If consuming one of the word's healthiest superfood raw is a bit difficult for you, then dehydrating them will make things much easier for you!

Prep time and cooking time: 10 hours | Serves: 4

Ingredients To Use:

- 1/4 teaspoon salt
- 1/2 lemon juice
- 2 tablespoons fresh cilantro, chopped
- 1/4 teaspoon cayenne pepper
- 4 avocados, halved and pitted

Step-by-Step Directions to cook it:

1. Cut your avocado into slices, drizzle lemon juice over avocado slices
2. Arrange the slices on cooking pan in a single layer
3. Transfer to your Omni Toaster Oven
4. Cook on Dehydrate Mode on 160 degrees F for 10 hours
5. Serve and enjoy once done!

Nutritional value per serving:

Calories: 412 kcal, Protein: 3g, Fat: 39g, Carbs: 17g

Chapter 10: Slow Cooking Recipes

Chia Pudding

Amazing slow cooker chia pudding, health over-dose in a cup!
Prep time and cooking time: 2 hours 10 minutes | Serves: 4

Ingredients To Use:

- 1/2 cup coconut chia granola
- 1/2 cup chia seeds
- 2 cups of coconut milk
- 2 tablespoons coconut, shredded and sweetened
- 1/4 cup maple syrup
- 1/2 teaspoon cinnamon powder
- 2 teaspoons cocoa powder
- 1/2 teaspoon vanilla extract

Step-by-Step Directions to cook it:

1. Add chia granola, chia seeds, coconut milk, maple syrup, coconut, cinnamon, cocoa powder and vanilla to your Omni Toaster Oven cooking basket
2. Cook on Slow Cook Mode on HIGH for 2 hours
3. Divide between serving bowls and enjoy!

Nutritional value per serving:

Calories: 201 kcal, Protein: 4g, Fat: 4g, Carbs: 11g

Chicken Omelet

Simple and delicate slow-cooked chicken omelet, just what bugs bunny needed!

Prep time and cooking time: 180 minutes | Serves: 4

Ingredients To Use:

- ounce rotisserie chicken, shredded
- 1 teaspoon mustard
- 1 tablespoon avocado mayonnaise
- 1 tomato, chopped
- 4 eggs, whisked
- 1 small avocado, pitted, peeled and chopped
- Pepper to taste

Step-by-Step Directions to cook it:

1. Take a bowl and add listed ingredients, toss well
2. Transfer to your Omni Toaster Oven
3. Cook in SLOW COOK mode on LOW for 3 hours
4. Serve and enjoy once done!

Nutritional value per serving:

Calories: 220 kcal, Protein: 6g, Fat: 9g, Carbs: 4g

Carrot And Pineapple Mix

The perfect combination of pineapple and carrot dish, just go ahead and give it a try, this is perfect of non-veg lovers!
Prep time and cooking time: 40 minutes | Serves: 4

Ingredients To Use:

- 1 cup raisins
- 6 cups of water
- 23 ounces natural applesauce
- 2 tablespoons stevia
- 2 tablespoons cinnamon powder
- 14 ounces carrots, shredded
- 8 ounces canned pineapple, crushed
- 1 tablespoon pumpkin pie spice

Step-by-Step Directions to cook it:

1. Add listed ingredients to a cooking basket
2. Transfer to your Omni Toaster Oven
3. Cook in SLOW COOK mode on LOW for 6 hours
4. Serve and enjoy!

Nutritional value per serving:

Calories: 170 kcal, Protein: 4g, Fat: 5g, Carbs: 15g

Wild Mushroom Pilaf

A health bowl of mushroom pilaf, you'll love it!
Prep time and cooking time: 3 hours | Serves: 4

Ingredients To Use:

- 1 cup wild rice
- 2 garlic cloves, minced
- 6 green onions, chopped
- 2 tablespoons olive oil
- 1/2 pound baby Bella mushrooms
- 2 cups of water

Step-by-Step Directions to cook it:

1. Add listed ingredients to a cooking basket, stir well
2. Transfer to your Omni Toaster Oven
3. Cook on in SLOW COOK mode on LOW for 3 hours
4. Serve and enjoy!

Nutritional value per serving:

Calories: 210 kcal, Protein: 4g, Fat: 7g, Carbs: 16g

Spinach And Bean Platter

A platter combo of bean and spinach, yum yum!
Prep time and cooking time: 4 hours | Serves: 4

Ingredients To Use:

- 5 carrots, sliced
- 1 and 1/2 cups great northern beans, dried
- 2 garlic cloves, minced
- 1 yellow onion, chopped
- Pepper to taste
- 1/2 teaspoon oregano, dried
- 5 ounces baby spinach
- 4 and 1/2 cups low sodium veggie stock
- 2 teaspoons lemon peel, grated
- 3 tablespoon lemon juice

Step-by-Step Directions to cook it:

1. Add beans, onion, carrot, oregano, and stock to your cooking basket
2. Stir well
3. Transfer to your Omni Air Fryer Toaster Oven
4. Cook on SLOW COOK mode for 4 hours on HIGH
5. Add spinach, lemon juice, and lemon peel
6. Stir and let it sit for 5 minutes more
7. Serve and enjoy!

Nutritional value per serving:

Calories: 219 kcal, Protein: 8g, Fat: 8g, Carbs: 14g

Acorn Mixed Platter

A very simple Acorn Squash, slow cooker, and fully packed with flavors!

Prep time and cooking time: 7 hours | Serves: 4

- 2 acorn squash, peeled and cut into wedges
- 16 ounces cranberry sauce, unsweetened
- 1/4 teaspoon cinnamon powder
- Pepper to taste

1. Add prepared according to wedges to your Cooking Basket
2. Add cranberry sauce, cinnamon, raisins, and pepper
3. Transfer to your Omni Toaster Oven
4. Cook on SLOW COOK mode on LOW for 7 hours
5. Serve and enjoy!

Calories: 200 kcal, Protein: 2g, Fat: 3g, Carbs: 15g

Italian Shrimp Salad

The Chef's Favorite Italian Shrimp Salad recipe, freshness in a bowl!
Prep time and cooking time: 8 hours | Serves: 4

Ingredients To Use:

- 4 cups low-sodium vegetable stock
- 2 tablespoons Italian seasoning
- 1 pound sausage, salt-free and sliced
- Pinch of black pepper
- 2 pounds shrimp, deveined
- 2 tablespoons parsley, chopped
- 4 tablespoons olive oil

Step-by-Step Directions to cook it:

1. Add stock, Italian seasoning, sausage, pepper, oil, shrimp to your Cooking Basket
2. Transfer to Omni Air Fryer Toaster Oven
3. Close the door
4. Cook on SLOW COOK mode in LOW for 8 hours
5. Add parsley, toss
6. Serve and enjoy!

Nutritional value per serving:

Calories: 202 kcal, Protein: 6g, Fat: 3g, Carbs: 14g

Potato Turkey Breast

Turkey breast packed with potatoes, a very delightful and health platter to try out!

Prep time and cooking time: 8 hours | Serves: 4

- 1/2 cup of cheese preferably shredded
- 1/4 tsp. of Italian seasoning
- 1 lb. ground beef
- 1 egg

Taco seasoning

- 1/2 tsp. of smoked paprika
- 1 tsp. of ground cumin
- 1/2 tsp. of garlic powder
- 1/4 tsp. of onion powder
- 1 tsp. of chili powder
- 1/4 tsp. of salt
- 1/2 tsp. of cocoa powder

Step-by-Step Directions to cook it:

1. Add turkey breast to your cooking basket
2. Add potatoes, cherries, water, onion, parsley, garlic, onion powder,r thyme, sage and paprika to the basket
3. Stir and season with pepper
4. Transfer to your Omni Air Frye Toaster Oven
5. Cook in SLOW COOK mode on LOW for 8 hours
6. Serve and enjoy!

Nutritional value per serving:

Calories: 220 kcal, Protein: 15g, Fat: 5g, Carbs: 8g

Juicy Slow Cooked Pork Roast

The most authentic Slow Cooked Pork Roast, just go ahead and give it a try, you won't be disappointed!
Prep time and cooking time: 8 hours | Serves: 4

Ingredients To Use:

- 2 pounds pork shoulder roast, boneless
- 1/3 cup low sodium vegetable stock
- 1/2 teaspoon garlic powder
- 1 tablespoon sage, dried
- 1/4 cup balsamic vinegar
- 1 tablespoon low sodium Worcestershire sauce
- 1 tablespoon honey

Step-by-Step Directions to cook it:

1. Add roast to cooking basket
2. Add stock
3. Take a bowl and add garlic powder, vinegar, Worcestershire sauce, honey and whisk well
4. Pour the mix over roast
5. Transfer to Omni Toaster oven
6. Cook on SLOW COOK mode on LOW for 8 hours
7. Once cooked, shred the meat, serve and enjoy the cooking juice!

Nutritional value per serving:

Calories: 214 kcal, Protein: 21g, Fat: 12g, Carbs: 5g

Traditional Greek Pork

We all know that the Greek's are some of the biggest health buffs out there! This Pork recipe the perfect representation of their culture!

Prep time and cooking time: 8 hours | Serves: 4

Ingredients To Use:

- 3 pounds pork shoulder, boneless
- 1/4 cup olive oil
- 2 teaspoons oregano, dried
- 1/4 cup lemon juice
- 2 teaspoons mustard
- 2 teaspoons mint
- 6 garlic clove, minced
- Pepper to taste

Step-by-Step Directions to cook it:

1. Take a bowl and add lemon juice, oregano, oil, mint, garlic, mustard, pepper and mix well
2. Rub the mix all over pork, cover and let it refrigerate for 1 day
3. Transfer to your cooking basket alongside marinade
4. Transfer to Omni Air Fryer Toaster Oven
5. Cook on SLOW COOK mode on LOW for 8 hours
6. Serve and enjoy once done!

Nutritional value per serving:

Calories: 260 kcal, Protein: 8g, Fat: 4g, Carbs: 14g

Chapter 11: Roasting Recipes

Bacon And Pepper Hash

Why not try out your roasting feature with some classic bacon and pepper hash? Stunning!

Prep time and cooking time: 30 minutes | Serves: 4

- 1 red bell pepper, diced
- 1 yellow onion, diced
- 1/2 pack uncooked bacon, diced
- 4 whole eggs
- 1 teaspoon salt
- 1 teaspoon celery salt
- 1 teaspoon black pepper
- 1 teaspoon paprika
- 2 zucchinis, peeled and diced

Step-by-Step Directions to cook it:

1. Add bacon to the Air Fryer basket. Set the Air Fryer basket inside the Omni toaster oven and close the lid.
2. Select the Roast mode at 300 degrees F temperature for 30 minutes. After 5 minutes, add zucchinis, onion, pepper, and spices to the Air Fryer basket. Toss well, then return the basket to the oven.
3. Beat eggs with salt and black pepper in a baking pan then toss in roasted veggies and bacon.
4. Place the pan in the Air Fryer toaster oven and close the lid. Cook for 5 minutes on Bake mode at 350 degrees F.
5. Serve and Enjoy!

Nutritional value per serving:

Calories: 286 kcal, Protein: 16g, Fat: 18g, Carbs: 4g

Authentic Gyro Chicken

The craziest Gyro chicken ever to bless the Omni appliance! Just roast it up, and you are good to go!
Prep time and cooking time: 40 minutes | Serves: 4

Ingredients To Use:

- 1 tablespoon Himalayan Salt
- 2 tablespoons new bay seasoning
- 2 tablespoons gyro seasoning
- 1 tablespoon avocado oil
- 2 pounds chicken thighs

Step-by-Step Directions to cook it:

1. Rub the chicken with avocado oil and all the spices liberally.
2. Place the gyro chicken in the Air Fryer basket.
3. Set the Air Fryer basket inside the Omni toaster oven and close the lid.
4. Select the Roast mode at 350 degrees F temperature for 25 minutes.
5. Flip the chicken when cooked halfway through and continue cooking. Serve warm.

Nutritional value per serving:

Calories: 375 kcal, Protein: 42g, Fat: 7g, Carbs: 0.7g

Hearty Indian Tandoori

The most authentic Tandoori chicken meal you can get!
Prep time and cooking time: 30 minutes + Chill time | Serves: 4

Ingredients To Use:

- 2 chicken leg with thighs

Marinade 2

- 2 teaspoons coriander powder
- 1 teaspoon black pepper
- 2 teaspoon dried Fenugreek seeds
- 1 pinch orange food color
- 4 tablespoons hung curd
- 1 teaspoon turmeric powder

- 2 teaspoon red chili powder
- 1 teaspoon Garam masala powder
- 1 teaspoon roasted cumin powder
- 2 tablespoons tandoori masala powder

Step-by-Step Directions to cook it:

1. Mix chicken with first marinade ingredients in a bowl and cover to marinate for 15 minutes.
2. Then stir in the rest of the second marinade ingredients and mix well. Cover the chicken and refrigerate for 12 hours approximately.
3. Place the tandoori chicken in a baking tray, lined with tin foil.
4. Set the Air Fryer basket inside the Omni Fryer toaster oven and close the lid.
5. Select the Roast mode at 300 degrees F temperature for 20 minutes. Serve warm.

Nutritional value per serving:

Calories: 385 kcal, Protein: 45g, Fat: 45g, Carbs: 7g

Must-Have Rotisserie Chicken

Thanks Giving night, but you are in a rush? Just cook up a Rotisserie Chicken, and you are good to go!

Prep time and cooking time: 60 minutes | Serves: 4

Ingredients To Use:

- 1/2 teaspoon dried thyme
- 1/2 teaspoon oregano
- 1/2 teaspoon dried basil
- 1/2 teaspoon paprika
- 1 teaspoon garlic powder
- 1 teaspoon fresh ground pepper
- 1 tablespoon salt
- 2 tablespoons avocado oil
- 5 pounds whole chicken, giblets removed

Step-by-Step Directions to cook it:

1. Brush the chicken with avocado oil and then rub the chicken liberally with all the spices.
2. Fix the Mix all the seasonings with oil to make a paste.
3. Place the chicken in a baking pan. Set the pan inside the Air Fryer toaster oven and close the lid.
4. Select the Roast mode at 360 degrees F temperature for 50 minutes. Serve warm.

Nutritional value per serving:

Calories: 350 kcal, Protein: 25g, Fat: 14g, Carbs: 5g

Bamboo Sprouts Roast

The Chinese Bamboo Sprouts recipe that you will fall in love with!
Prep time and cooking time: 25 minutes | Serves: 4

Ingredients To Use:

- 1 pound bamboo sprouts
- 2 tablespoons butter
- 1 cup parmesan cheese, grated
- 1/4 teaspoon paprika
- Salt and pepper to taste

Step-by-Step Directions to cook it:

1. Pre-heat your Omni Toaster Oven to 350 degrees F in Roast Mode
2. Take a baking dish and grease it well
3. Take a bowl and add butter, salt, pepper, paprika, and mix
4. Add bamboo to the butter marinade
5. Mix well
6. Marinate for 1 hour
7. Transfer to baking dish and Toast for 15 minutes
8. Serve and enjoy!

Nutritional value per serving:

Calories: 192 kcal, Protein: 12g, Fat: 15g, Carbs: 2g

Mixed Veggie Roast

An assorted collection of veggies roasted to perfection!
Prep time and cooking time: 20 minutes | Serves: 4

Ingredients To Use:

- 2 cups Roma tomatoes
- 1/2 cup mushrooms halved
- 1 red bell pepper, seeded and cut into bite-sized portions
- 1 tablespoon coconut oil
- 1 tablespoon garlic powder
- 1 teaspoon salt

Step-by-Step Directions to cook it:

1. Preheat your Omni Plus Toaster Oven 400 degrees F in Roast mode
2. Take a bowl and add mushrooms, Roma tomatoes, bell pepper, oil, salt, garlic powder and mix well
3. Transfer to Toaster Oven cooking basket
4. Cook for 12-15 minutes, making sure to shake occasionally
5. Serve and enjoy once crispy!

Nutritional value per serving:

Calories: 19 kcal, Protein: 7g, Fat: 16g, Carbs: 19g

Jalapeno Bacon Bombs

If you are craving for something a bit fatty, these spicy Bacon Bombs are just what the doctor ordered!

Prep time and cooking time: 30 minutes | Serves: 4

Ingredients To Use:

- 12 large jalapeno peppers
- 16 bacon strips
- 6 ounce of cashew cheese
- 2 teaspoon of garlic powder
- 1 teaspoon of chili powder

Step-by-Step Directions to cook it:

1. Preheat your Omni Toaster Oven to 350 degrees Fahrenheit in Roast
2. Place a wire rack over a roasting pan and keep it on the side
3. Make a slit lengthways across jalapeno pepper and scrape out the seeds, discard them
4. Place a nonstick skillet over high heat and add half of your bacon strip, cook until crispy
5. Drain them
6. Chop the cooked bacon strips and transfer to a large bowl
7. Add cashew cheese and mix
8. Season the cashew cheese and bacon mixture with garlic and chili powder
9. Mix well
10. Stuff the mix into the jalapeno peppers with and wrap raw bacon strip all around
11. Arrange the stuffed wrapped jalapeno on prepare wire rack
12. Toast for 10 minutes
13. Transfer to a cooling rack and serve!

Nutritional value per serving:

Calories: 209 kcal, Protein: 9g, Fat: 9g, Carbs: 15g

Roasted Cauliflower Bars

After the previous fat bomb, want to go for something a bit healthier? These Cauliflower Bars will satisfy your thirst!
Prep time and cooking time: 40 minutes | Serves: 4

Ingredients To Use:

- 1 cauliflower head, riced
- 12 cup low-fat mozzarella cheese, shredded
- 1/4 cup egg whites
- 1 teaspoon Italian dressing, low fat
- Pepper to taste

Step-by-Step Directions to cook it:

1. Spread cauliflower rice over a lined baking sheet
2. Pre-heat your Omni Toaster Oven for 375 degrees F in Roast Mode
3. Roast for 20 minutes
4. Transfer to a bowl and spread pepper, cheese, seasoning, egg whites and stir well
5. Spread in a rectangular pan and press
6. Transfer to Toaster Oven and cook for 20 minutes more
7. Serve and enjoy!

Nutritional value per serving:

Calories: 37 kcal, Protein: 1g, Fat: 3g, Carbs: 2g

Basil Dip And Vegetable Roast

Even if you hate vegetables, this basil dip will completely make a world of difference!

Prep time and cooking time: 35 minutes | Serves: 4

Ingredients To Use:

- 12 cherry tomatoes
- 3 slender zucchini, sliced into 1/2 inch thick rounds, cut into 24 pieces
- Salt as needed
- 1/4 cup olive oil
- 1 onion, quartered and cut into 24 pieces
- 2 red bell pepper, cut into 1-inch pieces, 12 pieces total

Basil dip

- 1/2 teaspoon salt
- 1/2 cup basil
- 1/2 cup extra virgin olive oil
- 1 cup zucchini, diced
- 1/2 cup raw walnuts

Step-by-Step Directions to cook it:

1. Preheat your Omni Plus Toaster Oven to 380 degrees F in Roast mode
2. Thread veggies into small skewers (small enough to fit in cooking basket)in a uniform pattern, place them on parchment pattern
3. The pattern should be tomatoes between 2 veggies
4. Apply oil all over and season well
5. Roast for 10-15 minutes

6. Once done, add dip ingredients to a food processor and process well
7. Add more olive oil if needed
8. Serve veggies with dip
9. Enjoy!

Calories: 112 kcal, Protein: 1g, Fat: 10g, Carbs: 4g

Spicy Orange Bowl

A bowl full of spice orange, what more could you ask for?
Prep time and cooking time: 40 minutes | Serves: 4

Ingredients To Use:

- 2 teaspoons sesame seed oil
- 1 date, pitted and soaked
- 3 tablespoons orange juice
- 1 tablespoon tamari
- 1 garlic clove, grated
- 1/2 teaspoon red chili flakes
- 1/2 teaspoon ginger, grated
- 1/2 teaspoon ginger, grated
- 1 tablespoon sesame seeds
- 2 cups zucchini, cubed

Step-by-Step Directions to cook it:

1. Preheat your Omni Toaster Oven to 380 degrees F
2. Add zucchini in cooking basket and drizzle oil on top
3. Roast for 10-20 minutes
4. Take your blender and add date, juice, tamari, garlic, flakes, ginger and pulse well
5. Put cooked zucchini to a skillet and add orange juice mixture to the pan, cook on a low simmer for 2-3 minutes until reduced
6. Serve and enjoy with a garnish of sesame seeds
7. Enjoy!

Nutritional value per serving:

Calories: 165 kcal, Protein: 6g, Fat: 13g, Carbs: 10g

Roasted Pork Tenderloin Roast

Premium and Juicy Pork Tenderloin Roast Dish right in your appliance, simple and fuss-free!
Prep time and cooking time: 40 minutes | Serves: 4

Ingredients To Use:

- 2 teaspoons sage, chopped
- Sunflower seeds and pepper
- 2 and1/2 pounds beef tenderloin
- 2 teaspoon thyme, chopped
- 2 garlic cloves, sliced
- 2 teaspoons rosemary, chopped
- 4 teaspoons olive oil

Step-by-Step Directions to cook it:

1. Preheat your Omni Toaster Oven to 425 degrees F in Roast mode
2. Take a small knife and cut incisions on tenderloin, insert one slice of garlic into the incision
3. Rub meat with oil
4. Take a bowl and add sunflower seeds, sage, thyme, rosemary, pepper and mix well
5. Rub spice mix over tenderloin
6. Put rubbed tenderloin into roasting pan and bake for 10 minutes
7. Lower temperature to 350 degrees F and cook for 20 minutes more until an internal thermometer read 145 degrees F
8. Transfer tenderloin to cutting board and let them sit for 15 minutes, slice into 20 pieces, and enjoy!

Nutritional value per serving:

Calories: 37 kcal, Protein: 1g, Fat: 3g, Carbs: 2g

Delicious Butterbean Rattatouille

This Ratatouille will completely remind you of the delicious ratatouille from the movie Ratatouille!

Prep time and cooking time: 50 minutes | Serves: 4

Ingredients To Use:

- 4 pieces of your favorite branded pork sausage
  For the ratatouille, you are going to be needing
- 1 finely chopped pepper
- 2 finely diced courgettes
- 1 diced aubergine
- 1 medium-sized diced red onion
- 1 tablespoon of olive oil
- Drained and rinsed 15 ounces of butter bean
- 1 tin of 15 ounce chopped tomatoes
- 2 sprigs of fresh thyme
- 1 tablespoon of balsamic vinegar
- 2 minced garlic cloves
- 1 finely chopped red chili

Step-by-Step Directions to cook it:

1. Pre-heat your Omni Toaster Oven to a temperature of 392 degrees Fahrenheit for about 3 minutes in Roast
2. Take out your cooking basket and add pepper, oil, aubergine, onion, courgettes and allow them to roast for 20 minutes
3. Give it a shake about halfway through
4. Remove the cooking basket and allow the content to cool
5. Lower down the temperature of your fryer to 356 degrees Fahrenheit

6. Take a saucepan and place it over medium heat and add the veggies alongside the remaining ingredients
7. Simmer the mixture for a while
8. Season with salt and pepper
9. Place the sausages into your Toaster Oven and cooking basket and cook for about 15 minutes, making sure to give them a shake
10. Take them out and serve with the prepared vegetables
11. Enjoy!

Nutritional value per serving:

Calories: 136 kcal, Protein: 4g, Fat: 4g, Carbs: 17g

Authentic Sirloin Roast Steak

Craving some steak? This Sirloin is just what you need!
Prep time and cooking time: 30 minutes | Serves: 4

Ingredients To Use:

- 4 small potatoes, chopped
- 1 tablespoon of Olive oil
- 1 teaspoon of Cayenne pepper
- 1 teaspoon of Italian herbs
- 1 teaspoon of Salt
- 70 ounce of Sirloin steak
- 1/2 a tablespoon of olive oil
- Salt as needed
- Pepper as needed

Step-by-Step Directions to cook it:

1. Take a medium-sized bowl and add olive oil, potatoes, Italian herbs, cayenne pepper and salt
2. Mix well
3. Pre-heat your Omni Toaster Oven to 356 degrees Fahrenheit in Roast mode
4. Place the potatoes in your Toaster Oven basket and cook for 16 minutes
5. Make sure to give the potatoes a toss halfway through
6. Once done, keep it on the side
7. Rub the steak with pepper, oil, and salt
8. Place the steak into your fryer and cook for 7-13 minutes at 392 Fahrenheit depending on your doneness
9. Serve with roasted potatoes, enjoy!

Nutritional value per serving:

Calories: 135 kcal, Protein: 23g, Fat: 5g, Carbs: 0g

Sriracha Satay Beef Roast

Bored with the traditional beef roast and want something a little bit more special? This Sriracha beef roast will set your world on fire!
Prep time and cooking time: 20 minutes | Serves: 4

Ingredients To Use:

- 1/4 cup roasted peanuts, chopped
- 1/2 cup cilantro, chopped
- 1 teaspoon ground coriander
- 1 teaspoon sriracha sauce
- 1 tablespoon sugar
- 1 tablespoon garlic, minced
- 1 tablespoons ginger, minced
- 1 tablespoons soy sauce
- 1 tablespoon fish sauce
- 2 tablespoon oil
- 1 pound beef shank flank steak, sliced

Step-by-Step Directions to cook it:

1. Whisk fish sauce with ginger, garlic, soy sauce, oil, sugar, coriander, 1/4 cup cilantro, and sriracha in a mixing bowl. Toss-in the beef strips and mix well to coat.
2. Cover the beef and refrigerate for 30 minutes. Place the beef in the cooking basket
3. Set the Air Fryer basket inside the Omni Plus Air Fryer toaster oven and close the lid. Select the Air Fry mode at 400 degrees F temperature for 8 minutes.
4. Flip the beef slices and continue cooking. Garnish with peanuts and cilantro. Serve warm.

Nutritional value per serving:

Calories: 390 kcal, Protein: 41g, Fat: 13g, Carbs: 8g

Classic Mediterranean Pork Delight

A pork dish with a Mediterranean twist, a fresh meal to roast!
Prep time and cooking time: 35 minutes | Serves: 4

Ingredients To Use:

- 4 pork chops, bone-in
- Salt and pepper to taste
- 1 teaspoon dried rosemary
- 3 garlic cloves, peeled and minced

Step-by-Step Directions to cook it:

1. Season pork chops with salt and pepper
2. Place in roasting pan
3. Add rosemary, garlic in a pan
4. Preheat your Omni Toaster oven to 425 degrees F in Roast Mode
5. Bake for 10 minutes
6. Lower heat to 350 degrees F
7. Roast for 25 minutes more
8. Slice pork and divide on plates
9. Drizzle pan juice all over
10. Serve and enjoy!

Nutritional value per serving:

Calories: 165 kcal, Protein: 26g, Fat: 2g, Carbs: 2g

Fennel And Artichoke Heart Roast

Artichoke hearts aren't generally that tasty, but the fennel really kicks things up a notch!

Prep time and cooking time: 40 minutes | Serves: 4

Ingredients To Use:

- 1 can whole artichoke hearts in water, drained and cut in half
- 1 fennel bulb, cut into wedges
- 2 tablespoons parsley, chopped
- 1 lemon juice
- 3 tablespoons extra virgin olive oil
- Salt and pepper, to taste

Step-by-Step Directions to cook it:

1. Preheat your Omni Toaster Oven to 425 degrees F in Roast mode
2. Take a bowl and place all ingredients
3. Toss to coat well
4. Arrange the vegetable on a baking sheet
5. Lined with aluminum foil
6. Toast for 25 minutes
7. Serve and enjoy!

Nutritional value per serving:

Calories: 95 kcal, Protein: 9g, Fat: 5g, Carbs: 5g

Roasted Mashed Celeriac

Tired of the same old mashed potatoes? Celiac is the way to go!
Prep time and cooking time: 30 minutes | Serves: 4

Ingredients To Use:

- 2 celeriac, washed, peeled and diced
- 2 teaspoons extra-virgin olive oil
- 1 tablespoon honey
- 1/2 teaspoon ground nutmeg
- Salt and pepper as needed

Step-by-Step Directions to cook it:

1. Pre-heat your Omni Toaster Oven to 400 degrees Fahrenheit in Roast mode
2. Line a baking sheet with aluminum foil and keep it on the side
3. Take a large bowl and toss celeriac and olive oil
4. Spread celeriac evenly on a baking sheet
5. Roast for 20 minutes until tender
6. Transfer to a large bowl
7. Add honey and nutmeg
8. Use a potato masher to mash the mixture until fluffy
9. Season with salt and pepper
10. Serve and enjoy!

Nutritional value per serving:

Calories: 136 kcal, Protein: 4g, Fat: 3g, Carbs: 26g

Carrot Soup Dish

This healthy carrot soup will just remind you of your grandmother!
Prep time and cooking time: 60 minutes | Serves: 4

Ingredients To Use:

- 8 large carrots, washed and peeled
- 6 tablespoons olive oil
- quart broth
- Cayenne pepper to taste
- Sunflower seeds and pepper to taste

Step-by-Step Directions to cook it:

1. Pre-heat your Omni Toaster Oven to 425 degrees F in Roast Mode
2. Take a baking sheet and add carrots, drizzle olive oil and roast for 30-45 minutes
3. Put roasted carrots into a blender and add broth, puree
4. Pour into saucepan and heat soup
5. Season with sunflower seeds, pepper, and cayenne
6. Drizzle olive oil
7. Serve and enjoy!

Nutritional value per serving:

Calories: 178 kcal, Protein: 25g, Fat: 25g, Carbs: 36g

Conclusion

I can't express how honored I am to think that you found my book interesting and informative enough to read it all through to the end.

I thank you again for purchasing this book and I hope that you had as much fun reading it as I had writing it.

I bid you farewell and encourage you to move forward with your Omni Plus Toaster Oven and fine your next culinary masterpiece!

CPSIA information can be obtained
at www.ICGtesting.com
Printed in the USA
LVHW020143141220
674086LV00030B/821

9 781954 294189